Corporate Short-Term Financing in Europe

Corporate Short-Term Financing in Europe: The Role of Trade Credit and Bank Loans in Liquidity Management offers a thorough analysis of how European companies manage liquidity, with a particular focus on trade credit and bank credit as key instruments. Drawing on rich cross-country data, this book examines the relationship between trade credit and short-term bank loans, analysing when firms substitute one for the other or use them together to optimise cash flow. With Europe's financial systems ranging from bank-based systems to market-driven economies, this study uncovers how firm size, industry and national context shape short-term financing strategies. The text also addresses how financial crises and regulatory shifts affect corporate short-term funding decisions. Combining theoretical frameworks with empirical evidence, this book provides fresh insights for academics, policymakers, financial managers and business leaders concerned with corporate liquidity, small- and medium-sized enterprise support and financial resilience and practitioners involved in credit risk assessment and working capital management. It is essential reading for anyone managing short-term corporate finance in today's fast-changing environment.

Julia Koralun-Bereźnicka is Associate Professor of Corporate Finance at the University of Gdańsk, Poland.

Routledge Focus on Economics and Finance

The fields of economics are constantly expanding and evolving. This growth presents challenges for readers trying to keep up with the latest important insights. Routledge Focus on Economics and Finance presents short books on the latest big topics, linking in with the most cutting-edge economics research.

Individually, each title in the series provides coverage of a key academic topic, whilst collectively the series forms a comprehensive collection across the whole spectrum of economics.

The Digital Transformation of Banking
Bilal Sucubaşı, Andrijana Bojadzievska Danevska, Savica Dimitrieska and Elena Parnardzieva Stanoevska

The Circular Economy and SMEs
Edited by Fahimeh Khatami

Financial Security and Household Life Insurance
Bridging the Gap
Joanna Dębicka and Anna Jędrzychowska

Corporate Short-Term Financing in Europe
The Role of Trade Credit and Bank Loans in Liquidity Management
Julia Koralun-Bereźnicka

For more information about this series, please visit: www.routledge.com/Routledge-Focus-on-Economics-and-Finance/book-series/RFEF

Corporate Short-Term Financing in Europe

The Role of Trade Credit and Bank Loans in Liquidity Management

Julia Koralun-Bereźnicka

Routledge
Taylor & Francis Group
LONDON AND NEW YORK

First published 2026
by Routledge
4 Park Square, Milton Park, Abingdon, Oxon OX14 4RN

and by Routledge
605 Third Avenue, New York, NY 10158

Routledge is an imprint of the Taylor & Francis Group, an informa business

British Library Cataloguing-in-Publication Data
A catalogue record for this book is available from the British Library

ISBN: 978-1-041-17103-4 (hbk)
ISBN: 978-1-041-17105-8 (pbk)
ISBN: 978-1-003-68798-6 (ebk)

DOI: 10.4324/9781003687986

Typeset in Times New Roman
by Newgen Publishing UK

Contents

Introduction *vii*

1 Theoretical aspects of corporate short-term finance 1
1.1 Overview of short-term financing sources 1
1.2 The role of trade credit in corporate finance 7
1.3 Short-term bank loans – function, availability, classification 18
1.4 Substitution and complementarity between trade credit and bank loans 23
1.5 Determinants of corporate short-term financing behaviour: from firm characteristics to industry and country contexts 29
1.6 Contemporary challenges to financial liquidity management 41

2 Trade credit vs. short-term bank loan: data and methods 66
2.1 Data characteristics 66
2.2 Definition of variables 69
2.3 Hypotheses' development 71
2.4 Research methods 81

3 Corporate short-term financing in Europe: a study of European companies 89
3.1 Descriptive statistics of corporate short-term finance behaviour 89
3.2 Complementary vs. substitution effect between trade credit and bank loan 99

3.3 Corporate short-term finance across size groups of firms 108
3.4 Corporate short-term finance across countries 113
3.5 Corporate short-term finance across industries 117

4 Conclusions 123

Index 129

Introduction

In the field of corporate finance, decisions concerning short-term financing represent some of the most immediate and operationally significant choices faced by firms. These decisions determine the liquidity and financial flexibility of firms, particularly in environments characterised by rapid change, competitive pressure and economic uncertainty. While long-term investment decisions often capture more attention in classical finance literature, short-term financing deserves equal attention due to its crucial role in ensuring firms' daily solvency and strategic responsiveness.

This book explores short-term financing decisions from a European perspective, offering a structured analysis of theoretical foundations, empirical determinants and practical patterns in financing behaviour. Europe provides a particularly rich context for such an investigation: its financial systems range from bank-based to market-oriented models, levels of capital market development differ markedly across countries and regulatory frameworks vary despite the policy harmonisation efforts of the European Union (EU). The EU, though unified in many policy areas, still exhibits significant heterogeneity in how businesses access and utilise short-term financing. This variety serves as a natural laboratory for comparative financial research.

The rationale for this study arises from the growing strategic relevance of short-term financial management in contemporary business practice. Firms operating in today's competitive global markets must constantly balance risk, return and liquidity. In this context, short-term financial management is not merely a technical necessity but a strategic function. The choice between trade credit and bank loans, the balance between internal and external funding and the use of financial instruments like factoring, leasing and commercial paper are all integral components of a firm's short-term financial policy. Despite their everyday relevance, these decisions remain under-researched, especially in cross-country, sector-specific and post-crisis contexts. Much of the existing literature is either country-specific or overly general in its treatment of short-term finance. This book addresses that gap by combining broad theoretical insights with fine-grained empirical analysis drawn from harmonised European company data.

Recent financial disruptions – most notably the global financial crisis of 2008 and the COVID-19 pandemic – have renewed academic interest in liquidity management and financial resilience. These episodes served as real-world stress tests for firms' short-term financial strategies, revealing vulnerabilities in conventional liquidity models and prompting urgent adjustments to shifting credit conditions, disrupted supply chains and unpredictable revenue streams. Previous studies highlight the increasing importance of multi-sourced liquidity solutions and document a range of adaptive practices, including the greater use of digital financing platforms, the strategic integration of treasury operations and diversification of funding sources. Such responses are associated with greater financial resilience and adaptability, offering important lessons for policymakers and corporate decision-makers in preparing for future periods of economic turbulence.

The primary objective of this book is to provide a comprehensive framework for understanding corporate short-term financing decisions, with an emphasis on the interaction between trade credit and short-term bank loans in European companies. Specifically, this book aims to:

1. Explore the theoretical foundations underlying trade credit, short-term borrowing and their interactions.
2. Review the determinants of short-term financial decisions, including firm-specific, sectoral and macroeconomic factors.
3. Examine the complementarity or substitutability between trade credit and short-term loans under different economic conditions.
4. Investigate the relative importance of country, industry and firm size in shaping the use of trade credit across European firms.
5. Assess the moderating role of country, industry and firm size in influencing the relationship between trade credit and both bank loans and other firm-specific determinants of short-term financing decisions.

The analysis draws upon a condensed, extensive literature review and empirical evidence derived from the BACH (2023) database, which aggregates standardised financial data for companies across 12 EU countries. Through this data, the study provides cross-sectional and longitudinal insights that enable robust hypothesis testing and the identification of behavioural patterns across different levels of firm characteristics and institutional contexts.

To meet these aims, the study combines conceptual and empirical approaches. The first part of this book is theoretical. It begins by examining foundational theories of short-term finance, including the financing advantage hypothesis, transaction cost economics and price discrimination theory, which together help explain the reasons behind firms' use of trade credit or bank loans. This theoretical exposition is followed by a critical review of empirical studies exploring how firm-level characteristics – such as size, profitability, asset structure – and contextual factors – like sectoral norms and institutional frameworks – shape short-term financing behaviour.

This theoretical basis provides the foundation for the empirical part of the study. The methodology, data structure and econometric models used are presented first, with regression techniques applied to assess how short-term financing decisions vary across firm size categories, industries and national contexts. The empirical analysis that follows evaluates the core question of whether trade credit and short-term loans operate as substitutes or complements and considers how this relationship responds to different structural and macroeconomic settings.

The European financial environment provides particularly favourable conditions for investigating short-term corporate financing decisions. Although EU-level initiatives such as the Capital Markets Union and the European Banking Union have sought to reduce national discrepancies, significant differences in credit access and financial practice continue to exist across member states. Bank-based systems, such as those in Germany and Austria, exemplify models where firms rely heavily on institutional lending, while other continental systems exhibit varying degrees of bank dependence and credit availability. In addition, firm size and industry type exert considerable influence over financing choices: small- and medium-sized enterprises (SMEs), which constitute the backbone of most European economies, often encounter more pronounced barriers to bank credit and thus rely more heavily on supplier financing. By contrast, larger or capital-intensive firms tend to enjoy greater access to institutional lending, owing to stronger collateral positions and established banking relationships.

The question of whether trade credit and bank loans function as substitutes or complements constitutes a key theme of this book's inquiry. The substitution hypothesis suggests that trade credit fills the gap when bank lending is restricted – an effect particularly evident in times of financial constraint or economic downturn. By contrast, the complementarity hypothesis holds that firms with better access to formal credit channels may also extend or use trade credit more extensively, thereby utilising both instruments as part of a broader liquidity strategy. The empirical analysis in this book tests both propositions across various firm sizes, sectors and national settings, generating insights into the complex nature of this financial relationship.

In advancing these findings, this book contributes to the broader corporate finance literature in several ways:

- It offers an integrated framework that connects theory, policy and empirical analysis on short-term financing.
- It provides one of the most comprehensive empirical studies to date using harmonised cross-country data from Europe.
- It advances understanding of how financing patterns shift in response to crises, regulatory changes and firm-specific dynamics.
- It provides guidance of practical value for financial managers, SMEs, policymakers and financial institutions regarding how to structure and employ short-term finance efficiently.

Furthermore, the focus on the relationship between trade credit and bank loans enriches the existing literature by emphasising the fluid and sometimes contradictory nature of financial decisions. In doing so, it challenges overly simplistic dichotomies and presents a more refined view of liquidity management in modern corporations.

The structure of this book reflects this dual focus. Chapter 1 develops the theoretical basis of corporate short-term finance, outlining the main instruments and the determinants of financing behaviour, while also addressing contemporary challenges to financial liquidity management. Chapter 2 presents the dataset, variable definitions, hypotheses and methodological framework employed in the empirical analysis. Chapter 3 discusses the empirical findings, focusing on descriptive patterns and testing the substitutive and complementary roles of trade credit and short-term bank loans across different firm sizes, industries and national contexts. The final section synthesises the results, considers their implications for theory and practice and outlines potential directions for future research.

In offering a coherent and empirically grounded account of corporate short-term finance, this book aims to contribute meaningfully to academic scholarship while also informing financial decision-makers and policymakers across diverse economic environments.

Reference

BACH (2023) *Bank for the Accounts of Companies Harmonized.* Available at: www.bach.banque-france.fr

1 Theoretical aspects of corporate short-term finance

1.1 Overview of short-term financing sources

Short-term financing plays an essential role in enabling companies to manage their immediate operational needs and maintain liquidity. It involves obtaining funds for a period typically less than one year to address requirements such as inventory purchases, payroll and other day-to-day expenditures. In the European context, businesses rely on various short-term financing options, each with unique characteristics, advantages and limitations. Distinguishing the specific features of these options enables effective financial management and informed short-term decision-making.

A defining feature of short-term financing is its brief duration, which aligns with the immediate requirements of corporate operations. Compared to long-term financing, it is often easier to obtain due to the lower risk it presents to lenders, given the shorter repayment period. This type of financing also tends to have lower interest rates, making it a cost-effective solution for companies seeking flexibility in responding to market conditions (Brealey, Myers and Allen, 2020). The accessibility and efficiency of short-term financing are crucial for supporting working capital management, enabling firms to optimise cash flows and respond to unforeseen financial demands (Petersen and Rajan, 1997).

Among the most widely utilised sources of short-term financing is **trade credit**, which refers to the arrangement where suppliers allow buyers to purchase goods or services on account, deferring payment to a later date. This form of financing is particularly popular among European firms as it facilitates smoother cash flow management without immediate cash outlay and due to its alignment with the cash

DOI: 10.4324/9781003687986-1

flow cycles of businesses. The terms of trade credit, such as the credit period and any discounts for early payment, are typically negotiated between the buyer and supplier. Suppliers often extend trade credit to strengthen long-term relationships and encourage repeat business, although excessive reliance can strain supplier relationships and hinder firms' ability to take advantage of early payment discounts (Ferrando and Mulier, 2013). Trade credit usage also varies significantly across industries and firm sizes, with larger firms generally receiving more favourable terms due to their bargaining power (Afrifa *et al.*, 2023). While trade credit is a convenient financing source, overreliance can strain supplier relationships and may lead to missed discount opportunities.

Commercial bank loans represent another essential short-term financing option. Commercial banks offer various short-term loan products, including lines of credit, overdrafts and term loans, to meet the immediate financing needs of businesses. These loans provide companies with the necessary funds to manage working capital, inventory and other short-term obligations. The accessibility and terms of bank loans depend on factors such as the company's creditworthiness, financial health and the prevailing economic environment. In Europe, bank loans remain a dominant source of short-term funding, particularly for small and medium-sized enterprises (SMEs), which often rely on them to manage liquidity constraints and operational continuity (Beck, Demirgüç-Kunt and Maksimovic, 2008). However, the relative cost of bank loans can be higher for SMEs due to their perceived risk, making access more challenging compared to larger firms with stronger credit profiles (Andrieu, Staglianòa and van der Zwan, 2018). The role of bank loans and trade credit in financing SMEs has been extensively analysed, with studies suggesting that their usage depends on firm-specific and macroeconomic conditions (Palacín-Sánchez, Canto-Cuevas and Di-Pietro, 2019; Pinto, Henriques, Cardoso, *et al.*, 2023). Smaller firms often rely on trade credit due to restricted bank loan access, highlighting its role as an alternative liquidity source (Bussoli and Marino, 2018).

Commercial paper offers a feasible alternative for large, financially stable corporations with high credit ratings. Commercial paper is an unsecured, short-term debt instrument issued by corporations to finance their short-term liabilities. This type of debt instrument provides firms with the ability to raise funds at relatively low interest rates in financial markets. However, typically, only companies with robust credit profiles have access to this funding mechanism. In Europe, the commercial paper market is well-regulated to maintain stability and its use is primarily limited to firms with robust financial structures. The commercial paper market provides an alternative to bank loans, offering potentially lower borrowing costs and diversification of funding sources. However, the market's accessibility can be influenced by economic conditions and investor confidence. Despite its advantages, commercial paper is highly sensitive to market conditions and its availability can diminish during periods of economic uncertainty (Diamond, 1991).

In addition to traditional sources, alternative financing options such as factoring and money market funds (MMFs) have gained widespread acceptance. **Factoring** is a financial arrangement in which a firm sells its accounts receivable to a third-party factor in exchange for immediate cash – typically at a discounted rate. This process enables companies to convert outstanding invoices into liquid funds, thereby easing working capital constraints and mitigating liquidity risks. Factoring is especially helpful for SMEs or firms with volatile cash flows, as it provides a means to finance operations without incurring additional debt. The decision to use factoring is often driven by a demand for asset-based financing, particularly among small firms, rather than organisational restructuring strategies (Summers and Wilson, 2000). The practice can be structured as either recourse or non-recourse factoring, with non-recourse arrangements transferring a greater portion of the credit risk to the factor, although at a higher cost. In addition to providing immediate liquidity, factors often offer credit assessment and collection services, which can help companies manage customer defaults more efficiently. However, the discount rates applied by factors may reduce overall profit margins and reliance on factoring might signal financial weakness to external stakeholders (Mian and Smith Jr., 1992; Fisman and Love, 2003). This method is therefore best suited for firms that need a rapid cash inflow and are willing to trade off some profitability for improved liquidity.

In contrast, MMFs offer a low-risk option for managing surplus cash while ensuring daily liquidity. MMFs are investment vehicles that offer businesses a relatively safe and short-term investment option for surplus cash. These funds invest in high-quality, short-term debt instruments such as treasury bills, commercial paper and certificates of deposit, thereby preserving capital while generating modest returns. Managed by professional portfolio managers, MMFs diversify their investments across various instruments to minimise risk, making them an attractive financing instrument for companies seeking to optimise their short-term cash management. Although the returns from MMFs are generally lower compared to higher-risk investments, the emphasis on safety and liquidity is particularly valuable during periods of market uncertainty or economic downturns. Moreover, the performance of these funds is closely tied to central bank policies and prevailing interest rates, which can influence both the yield and stability of returns (Opler *et al.*, 1999; Brealey, Myers and Allen, 2020). In the European Union, MMFs are regulated to ensure stability and reduce systemic risk, making them a reliable short-term financing source for companies. As firms increasingly seek to balance risk and reward in managing excess liquidity, MMFs have emerged as a key component of short-term financial strategy.

Complementing these options, **private credit** providers have significantly expanded the short-term financing instruments, especially in the wake of tighter bank lending standards following the global financial crisis (GFC). Private credit involves non-bank institutions providing loans or credit facilities to companies. Unlike traditional banks, private credit providers – including specialty lenders, private equity-backed funds and business development companies – offer specific financing solutions designed to meet the unique needs of firms that may struggle to access conventional bank loans. These providers offer greater flexibility in terms of covenant structures and repayment schedules, often processing applications more quickly than traditional financial institutions. However, this flexibility comes at a cost; the interest rates charged by private credit providers tend to be higher due to the increased risk associated with lending to borrowers with limited credit histories or insufficient collateral. Despite these higher costs, the customised nature of private credit makes it a helpful tool for companies operating in niche markets or those requiring innovative financing arrangements. The market has been expanding in Europe, with private credit groups increasingly participating in financing needs traditionally served by banks. This segment of financing thus represents a crucial alternative for firms seeking to bridge the gap between traditional financing and their immediate cash flow needs (Beck, Demirgüç-Kunt and Maksimovic, 2008; Ferrando and Mulier, 2013).

Informal lending represents another considerable source of short-term financing, particularly for small businesses and firms operating in developing economies. Unlike formal bank loans, informal lending involves borrowing from family, friends, private moneylenders, or community financing groups. This type of financing is often characterised by flexible repayment terms, lower administrative requirements and faster access to funds compared to traditional credit sources (Tomy and Wittenberg-Moerman, 2024). Although informal lending can provide crucial liquidity, it also carries risks such as higher interest rates from private lenders and the potential for strained personal relationships (Weining, Jian and Shubhranshu, 2017). Furthermore, informal credit markets often lack legal protections, making enforcement mechanisms weaker compared to formal financial institutions. However, studies suggest that informal lending plays a stabilising role in credit-constrained environments, serving as a vital funding option when formal financial systems fail to meet business needs (Salcedo-Pérez and Patiño, 2017).

The choice of short-term financing source depends on various factors, including cost, accessibility and regulatory considerations. Trade credit and commercial paper generally offer lower costs but require strong creditworthiness, while bank loans and private credit are more accessible to smaller firms but often come with higher interest rates. Macroeconomic conditions and regulatory frameworks further shape the availability and attractiveness of these options. For instance, stricter banking regulations implemented as a result of financial crises might increase firms' reliance on non-bank financing (Carbo-Valverde, Udell and Rodríguez-Fernández, 2011). Understanding the various short-term financing options available is crucial for firms to optimise liquidity management and maintain operational stability. Table 1.1 provides an overview of short-term financing options available to companies, summarising their main features, advantages and disadvantages.

The European short-term financing environment is evolving, shaped by regulatory changes, economic conditions and market dynamics. Stricter banking regulations have contributed to the growth of private credit, signalling a shift towards alternative financing sources. Simultaneously, the integration of financial markets within the EU aims to enhance the availability and efficiency of short-term financing options for businesses across member states. In this context, short-term financing remains indispensable for sustaining operations and addressing liquidity challenges. European companies have access to a diverse range of options, including trade credit, bank

Table 1.1 Overview of short-term financing options

Financing option	*Main Features*	*Advantages*	*Disadvantages*
Trade credit	Supplier extends credit for purchases	– no or low interest cost, – strengthens supplier relationships	– may limit purchasing power, – potential loss of early payment discounts
Bank loans	Short-term loans, overdrafts, credit lines	– structured repayment, – available for SMEs	– higher cost for SMEs, – requires credit assessment
Commercial paper	Unsecured short-term corporate debt	– lower interest rates for large firms, – quick access to funds	– limited to creditworthy firms, – sensitive to market conditions
Factoring	Selling accounts receivable for immediate cash	– provides quick liquidity, – reduces credit risk	– higher financing cost, – loss of receivables control
Money market funds	Investment vehicle for short-term cash	– low-risk liquidity management option	– lower returns compared to other financing sources
Private credit	Non-bank institutions offering customised loans	– flexible terms, – faster processing	– higher costs, – less regulatory oversight
Informal lending	Borrowing from family, friends, or private lenders	– quick access, – flexible terms	– higher risk, – lack of legal protections

Sources: Own compilation based on: Diamond (1991); Mian and Smith (1992); Petersen and Rajan (1997); Opler *et al.* (1999); Fisman and Love (2003); Beck, Demirgüç-Kunt and Maksimovic (2008); Ferrando and Mulier (2013); Salcedo-Pérez and Patiño (2017); Weining, Jian and Shubhranshu (2017); Andrieu, Staglianò and van der Zwan (2018); Brealey, Myers and Allen (2020); Afrifa *et al.* (2023); Tomy and Wittenberg-Moerman (2024).

loans and commercial paper, each suited to specific financial needs and circumstances. The ongoing evolution of financial markets not only influences the availability and cost of these financing sources but also shows the need to distinguish their characteristics, benefits and limitations. By carefully evaluating these factors, businesses can make informed decisions that effectively manage liquidity, align with their financial strategies and adapt to dynamic market conditions.

1.2 The role of trade credit in corporate finance

Trade credit plays a significant role in corporate finance, serving as an essential mechanism for managing short-term liquidity and mitigating financial constraints. It enables firms to acquire goods and services without immediate cash payment, thus easing cash flow pressures and increasing operational flexibility. Its significance can be proven by the widespread use of trade credit across economies, particularly by firms that encounter difficulties in obtaining alternative sources of finance (Abuhommous, 2017). In contrast to bank loans, trade credit is inherently integrated into business transactions, reflecting the mutual trust between suppliers and buyers (Petersen and Rajan, 1997).

Theoretical frameworks provide explanations for why firms engage in trade credit arrangements as part of their short-term financing strategies. Petersen and Rajan (1997) classify these motivations into three broad categories: transaction cost, financing advantage and price discrimination theories.

A key contribution to the transaction cost perspective is made by Ferris (1981), who proposes that trade credit allows firms to consolidate multiple payments for deliveries into a single periodic obligation. This separates the timing of deliveries from the payment schedule, helping firms manage inventories and liquidity more efficiently. Trade credit thus reduces the operational costs associated with frequent, uncertain transactions.

The financing advantage theory states that suppliers hold informational advantages over financial institutions in assessing their customers' creditworthiness, thereby enabling more efficient lending (Smith, 1987; Mian and Smith, 1992). Suppliers can more easily monitor, repossess and even resell goods if a customer defaults, which lowers enforcement costs. Biais and Gollier (1997) extend this by showing that trade credit mitigates information asymmetries, while Burkart and Ellingsen (2004) argue it can even complement bank financing by enhancing customer credit profiles.

The price discrimination theory, first formalised by Meltzer (1960), views trade credit as a tool for differentiating among customers based on risk. Creditworthy customers pay promptly to obtain discounts, while riskier firms, unable to secure cheaper financing elsewhere, opt for delayed payment. Suppliers may strategically extend credit to such firms to protect their own long-term interests, particularly when they rely on them for future sales. Empirical findings by Nilsen (2002) support this view, especially during periods of tight monetary conditions.

These theoretical perspectives provide a multidimensional understanding of trade credit, highlighting its role not just as a liquidity tool, but also as a mechanism for managing uncertainty, addressing information asymmetries and strategically pricing customer relationships.

Trade credit represents an essential dimension of short-term corporate finance, often interacting closely with bank loans to shape firms' liquidity strategies. Before examining its historical development, financial rationale and strategic implications, it is useful to observe how trade credit usage, represented by accounts, payable compares with short-term bank loans across different contexts. Figures 1.1–1.3 provide an overview of these relationships in Europe by country, firm size and industry, respectively.

As shown in Figure 1.1, the average ratio of trade credit to total assets ranges from about 12% in Italy to 13.2% in Poland. Short-term bank loans, by contrast, remain relatively stable across countries, varying between approximately 5.2% (e.g., Austria, France) and 5.5% (Luxembourg, Poland, Slovakia). This narrow spread in short-term bank loans suggests that formal bank credit availability is broadly comparable in the sample, whereas the modestly higher payables

Figure 1.1 Trade credit vs. short-term bank loans by country.

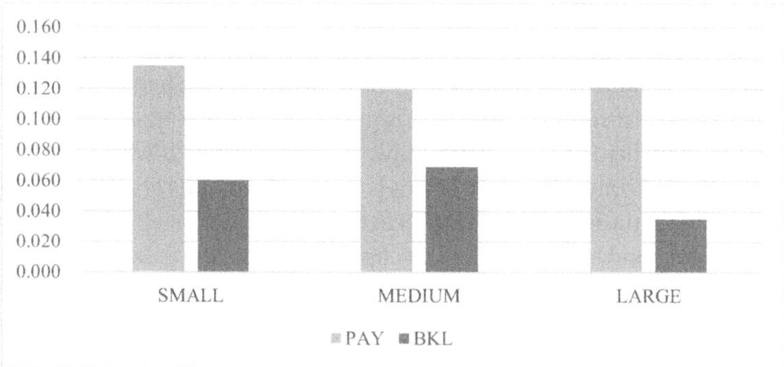

Figure 1.2 Trade credit vs. short-term bank loans by firm size.

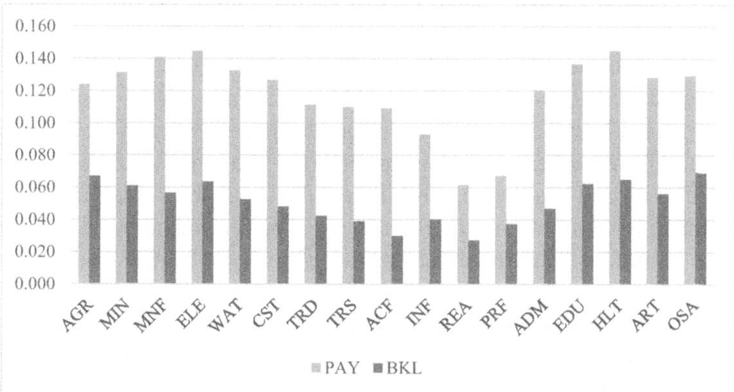

Figure 1.3 Trade credit vs. short-term bank loans by industry.

ratios in certain economies (e.g., Poland, Portugal, Spain) may reflect structural preferences for supplier financing or differences in banking regulations and credit cultures. Nonetheless, no country displays an extreme imbalance between the two financing forms, which indicates a generally consistent reliance on both trade credit and short-term bank loans across the considered European countries.

Figure 1.2 reveals distinct financing patterns across firm size groups. Small firms exhibit the highest average trade credit ratio at

13.5%, suggesting a greater reliance on supplier financing, likely due to more limited access to formal bank credit. Medium firms show a slightly lower payables ratio (12%) but the highest bank loan ratio at almost 7%, indicating that these firms tend to leverage bank credit more intensively. In contrast, large firms maintain a similar trade credit ratio to medium firms (12.1%) yet have a considerably lower bank loan ratio (3.5%). Interestingly, although one might intuitively expect large firms to obtain bank loans more easily due to their established creditworthiness and broader access to capital markets, the data indicate that large firms rely less on short-term bank loans. This may suggest that large firms have access to a wider selection of financing instruments, reducing their dependency on traditional bank credit. Overall, these differences highlight how firm size influences the balance between trade credit and bank financing, with smaller companies leaning more heavily on supplier credit, medium-sized firms relying more on bank loans and large firms utilising a diversified financing mix.

This cross-industry analysis reveals the highest variation in financing patterns compared to the more uniform differences observed across countries (Figure 1.1) and firm sizes (Figure 1.2). Figure 1.3 illustrates that, across various industries, trade credit consistently represents a higher proportion of assets than short-term bank loans, although the extent varies by sector. For example, sectors such as electricity and healthcare exhibit the highest payables ratios at 14.5%, indicating a pronounced reliance on supplier financing. Similarly, the manufacturing sector shows a relatively elevated trade credit ratio (14.1%), accompanied by a moderate bank loans ratio (5.6%), suggesting that firms in this industry significantly prefer trade credit over bank loans. In contrast, sectors like real estate and professional services present the lowest payables ratios (6.2% and 6.7%, respectively), which might reflect either a lower dependency on trade credit or a greater use of alternative financing mechanisms. Additionally, industries such as accommodation and food display the lowest bank loans ratio (3%), possibly indicating limited access to or a reduced emphasis on bank financing. These variations reveal how industry-specific factors – such as production cycles, asset tangibility and operational requirements –shape financing strategies, leading to varied relation between trade credit and bank loans across sectors.

Trade credit has a long historical precedent, dating back to ancient civilisations where merchants engaged in barter-based transactions before transitioning to deferred payments (Chapman, 1984). During the medieval period, trade credit became formalised through promissory notes and bills of exchange, facilitating commercial transactions across expanding trade routes. By the 19th and early 20th centuries, industrialisation accelerated the widespread use of trade credit, particularly in manufacturing and wholesale sectors, as firms sought to balance production cycles with cash inflows (Accominotti and Ugolini, 2019). In contemporary corporate finance, trade credit has gained increasing relevance as firms strategically manage liquidity, leveraging supplier financing as an alternative to bank loans (Petersen and Rajan, 1997). This shift has been particularly remarkable during financial crises, where access to formal credit is constrained, prompting firms to rely more heavily on supplier credit to sustain operations (Carbó-Valverde, Rodríguez-Fernández and Udell, 2016). The continued integration of digital trade finance solutions and fintech innovations has further transformed trade credit into a dynamic financing tool that enhances financial flexibility and efficiency in modern supply chains (Bastos and Pindado, 2013).

A critical aspect of trade credit in corporate finance is its dual role – both as trade credit granted (offered by firms to their customers) and trade credit received (obtained by firms from their suppliers). These two perspectives – summarised in Table 1.2 – have distinct financial implications. When a firm grants trade credit, it acts as a financier, extending payment terms to customers to facilitate sales and

Table 1.2 The dual role of trade credit in corporate finance

Aspect	*Role of trade credit*	
	Granted (Receivables)	*Received (Payables)*
Function	Financing customers to stimulate sales and loyalty	Obtaining supplier financing to improve liquidity
Financial impact	Increases accounts receivable and ties up capital	Reduces immediate cash outflow and improves cash flow
Risk	Default risk from customers, delayed payments	Dependency risk on supplier credit availability
Strategic use	Competitive advantage, customer retention	Short-term financing alternative to bank loans
Monitoring role	Enables firms to assess customer creditworthiness	Allows suppliers to monitor firm financial health

Sources: Own compilation based on: Deloof and Jegers (1999); Cuñat (2007); Bougheas, Mateut and Mizen (2009).

strengthen business relationships. Conversely, when a firm receives trade credit, it benefits from deferred payments, which can improve cash flow and liquidity management (Deloof and Jegers, 1999). However, granting trade credit also exposes firms to liquidity risks by tying up capital in accounts receivable, potentially limiting their ability to fund operations and invest in growth opportunities.

Trade credit typically operates through an agreement where a supplier offers goods or services to a buyer on credit, allowing payment at a later date rather than requiring immediate cash settlement (Ng, Smith and Smith, 1999). The most common payment terms include net 30, net 60 and net 90, meaning payment is due within 30, 60, or 90 days, respectively (Wilner, 2000). Many suppliers incentivise early payments by offering discounts, such as '2/10, net 30', which means a buyer receives a 2% discount if payment is made within 10 days; otherwise, the full amount is due in 30 days (Wilson and Summers, 2002). Conversely, late payments may incur penalties or interest charges, depending on the agreement. Trade credit is also structured through open accounts, where goods are delivered before payment, or promissory notes, which involve formalised commitments to pay at a specified date (Cuñat, 2007). This mechanism provides financial flexibility to buyers while helping suppliers maintain long-term commercial relationships and stable revenue streams (Bougheas, Mateut and Mizen, 2009).

A critical aspect of trade credit in corporate finance is its function as a substitute or complement to bank financing. Empirical evidence suggests that firms with restricted access to bank loans often resort to trade credit to finance working capital needs (Atanasova, 2007). This is particularly pronounced during periods of financial distress when credit markets tighten and traditional lending becomes constrained (Love, Preve and Sarria-Allende, 2007). Conversely, firms with strong banking relationships may still utilise trade credit as a supplementary source of finance to optimise liquidity management (Afrifa *et al.*, 2023). The substitution versus complementarity debate remains an active area of research, with studies highlighting the complex relationship between trade credit and institutional finance (McGuinness and Hogan, 2014).

The financial rationale behind trade credit extends beyond mere liquidity support. Suppliers often extend credit not solely for financial intermediation but also as a strategic tool to strengthen customer loyalty and enhance market competitiveness (Agostino and Trivieri, 2014). The provision of trade credit can serve as a signal of product quality, with longer credit terms indicating confidence in the durability and reliability of goods (Deloof and Jegers, 1996). Furthermore, trade credit terms can be used to price discriminate among buyers, allowing suppliers to adjust payment conditions based on customer creditworthiness and transaction histories (Biais and Gollier, 1997). At the same time, firms granting trade credit may use it strategically to maintain bargaining power over their customers, securing long-term business relationships.

From a corporate finance perspective, the impact of trade credit on firm profitability is a subject of considerable interest. While trade credit facilitates operational efficiency by enabling firms to manage their cash conversion cycles effectively, excessive reliance on supplier credit can lead to financial vulnerabilities (Abuhommous, 2017). Additionally, research suggests that trade credit plays a role in corporate cost behaviour, as firms adjust their financial strategies in response to credit availability, impacting overall cost management and efficiency (Costa and Habib, 2021). Firms with prolonged trade credit dependence may experience increased financial distress, particularly if suppliers impose stricter repayment conditions or withdraw credit lines abruptly (Molina and Preve, 2012). Conversely, firms that grant too much trade credit without sufficient risk assessment may suffer from bad debts, increased financial pressure and reduced profitability. This indicates the need for firms to maintain a balanced approach in leveraging trade credit without overextending liabilities.

Trade credit is also closely linked to creditworthiness and financial signalling. Firms with strong financial health often receive favourable credit terms, whereas those with weaker financial positions may encounter restrictive conditions or even credit rationing (Ahmed, Xiaofeng and Khalid, 2014). In some cases, suppliers act as alternative lenders, assessing buyer creditworthiness through non-traditional metrics, such as payment history and order volumes (Cai, Chen and Xiao, 2014). This informal credit assessment mechanism differentiates trade credit from bank financing, where lending decisions are typically based on formal financial metrics and collateral requirements (Bougheas, Mateut and Mizen, 2009). Similarly, firms granting trade credit must continuously monitor their customers' financial stability to minimise the risk of non-payment, ensuring that their accounts receivable remain viable assets rather than financial burdens.

From the borrower's perspective, the comparatively flexible monitoring practices of suppliers – as opposed to the stricter bank procedures – can be particularly advantageous. Huyghebaert (2006), in a study of Belgian start-ups, found that entrepreneurs often prefer trade credit because suppliers are generally more lenient than banks during periods of financial distress. The study shows that ongoing commercial relationships and transaction frequency provide suppliers with informal mechanisms to assess risk, allowing them to extend credit even when traditional lenders are reluctant. This supplier tolerance offers an alternative source of financing for young firms facing constrained access to formal credit markets.

Beyond its function as a financing tool, trade credit also serves as an informal monitoring mechanism, reducing information asymmetry between suppliers and buyers. Since suppliers typically have repeated transactions with buyers, they are well-positioned to observe financial behaviour, inventory turnover and overall business performance (Smith, 1987). Unlike banks, which rely on periodic financial disclosures, suppliers receive real-time insights into a firm's liquidity position through order frequency, payment delays and changes in purchasing behaviour (Petersen and Rajan, 1997). This enables suppliers to dynamically adjust credit terms based on perceived risks, effectively acting as a substitute for financial intermediaries (Biais and Gollier, 1997). Furthermore, empirical studies suggest that suppliers enforce discipline by threatening to cut off credit or delay shipments in cases of persistent payment issues, thereby incentivising buyers to maintain sound financial practices (Wilner, 2000). This implicit monitoring role not only mitigates default risk for suppliers but also enhances overall credit discipline within supply chains (Cuñat, 2007). Likewise, firms that grant trade credit can use payment behaviours as a tool to assess customer reliability and adjust future credit terms accordingly.

Additionally, firms with weak banking relationships often find trade credit to be an essential bridge to formal financing, as consistent supplier payments can improve their creditworthiness in the eyes of financial institutions (Ng, Smith and Smith, 1999). Thus, trade credit plays a crucial role in corporate governance by improving financial transparency and accountability within business networks.

In the context of supply chain financing, trade credit facilitates smoother transactions between firms and suppliers, ensuring continuity in purchasing and inventory management. Efficient trade credit management enhances supply chain resilience, particularly in volatile market conditions where firms face liquidity constraints (Barrot, 2016). However, extended payment terms may create cash flow pressures for suppliers, necessitating the use of factoring or trade credit insurance to mitigate default risks (Summers and Wilson, 2003). The role of trade credit in supply chains highlights its dual function as both a financial tool and a relational instrument between businesses (Cuñat, 2007). At the same time, firms that extend trade credit must ensure that their receivables are managed effectively to prevent cash flow shortages that could impact their operational stability.

Recent technological advancements have influenced the evolution of trade credit, with digital platforms and fintech innovations streamlining credit assessment and transaction processes (Liu and Wang, 2023). The integration of blockchain and artificial intelligence in trade credit management has enhanced transparency and efficiency, reducing risks associated with late payments and credit defaults (Shi, 2022). Furthermore, regulatory changes aimed at improving payment practices and reducing supplier risks have shaped trade credit policies across different jurisdictions (Belghitar and Mateus, 2016). These developments show the ongoing transformation of trade credit as a dynamic component of corporate finance.

Trade credit has been shown to play a crucial role in economic crises, as evidenced by its function in stabilising firms during the 2008 financial crisis and the COVID-19 pandemic (Bastos and Pindado, 2013). During these periods, access to traditional credit sources became constrained, leading firms to increasingly rely on supplier financing as a liquidity buffer (Demir and Javorcik, 2020). Studies suggest that trade credit acts as a counter-cyclical financing tool, with increased usage during economic downturns when banks implement stricter lending policies (Hui, Xiaojun and Shunming, 2011). During financial downturns, trade credit often substitutes for bank financing when credit markets tighten (Casey and O'Toole, 2014; Bussoli and Marino, 2018). Research on European SMEs confirms that trade credit serves as a sustainable financing mechanism, ensuring firms' operational continuity during crises (Canto-Cuevas, Palacín-Sánchez and Di Pietro, 2016; Afrifa *et al.*, 2023). However, prolonged economic distress can also lead to an accumulation of unpaid invoices, intensifying financial instability within supply chains (Luo, 2022).

Apart from its role as a financing mechanism, trade credit also serves an important signalling function in financial markets. Empirical studies suggest that suppliers' willingness to extend trade credit signals to banks that a firm is creditworthy, especially when conventional financial information is insufficient or unavailable. This is particularly relevant for new firms that have yet to establish strong relationships with banks. Banks may view trade credit as an indicator of a firm's reliability and financial health, using it as supplementary information to assess lending decisions (Biais and Gollier, 1997; Burkart and Ellingsen, 2004). Agostino and Trivieri (2014) provide evidence that trade credit is an important source of information for banks, particularly in the early stages of bank–firm relationships when traditional financial metrics are not well-established. Their findings suggest that firms that can obtain trade credit may find it easier to access bank loans in the future, as banks perceive supplier credit as a confirmation of a firm's creditworthiness. Additionally, even after several years of lending relationships, banks continue to consider suppliers as reliable sources of information on firms' financial conditions. This indicates that the role of trade credit is dual. It serves not only as a financing mechanism but also as a means of reducing information asymmetry between borrowers and lenders, thus facilitating access to institutional funding.

In addition to its liquidity and signalling roles, trade credit also contributes to reducing treasury uncertainties (Brennan, Maksimovics and Zechner, 1988). By allowing deferred payments, trade credit creates a buffer that smooths cash outflows and provides predictability in managing working capital, especially in periods of fluctuating revenues or seasonal demand. This stabilising effect can be particularly appreciated by firms operating in uncertain environments, as it reduces the need for continuous short-term liquidity forecasting.

Moreover, trade credit offers distinct control benefits during the early stages of a firm's development. Unlike bank loans, which often involve restrictive covenants and formal monitoring, trade credit is more flexible and less invasive. It allows new ventures to maintain greater control over their operations and strategic decisions while still accessing essential resources. Suppliers, relying on relational information and trust-based assessments, may offer more favourable terms to new firms, making trade credit a crucial financing channel during the initial growth phase (Huyghebaert, Van De Gucht and Van Hulle, 2007).

Another crucial dimension of trade credit is its role in corporate governance and financial transparency. Research indicates that firms with strong governance structures are more likely to engage in responsible trade credit practices, ensuring timely payments and minimising default risks (Cowton and San-Jose, 2017). On the contrary, firms with unclear financial reporting may use trade credit as a means of hiding liquidity constraints, raising concerns among suppliers regarding payment reliability (Fabbri and Klapper, 2016). This also reveals the importance of information asymmetry in trade credit relationships, where firms with credible financial disclosures are more likely to secure favourable credit terms (Giannetti, Burkart and Ellingsen, 2011).

Geographically, the use of trade credit varies across regions, influenced by institutional frameworks, banking sector development and cultural factors (Belghitar and Mateus, 2016). European firms, for instance, exhibit higher trade credit reliance compared to their counterparts in the United States, reflecting differences in financial market structures and business practices (Mateut and Mizen, 2003; Cantero Sáiz *et al.*, 2017). In emerging markets, trade credit plays a particularly considerable role in supporting SMEs that face limited access to formal financial institutions (Rahman, Rozsa and Cepel, 2018). Understanding these regional disparities is essential for policymakers seeking to improve trade credit availability and financial stability.

Future research may further explore the evolving role of trade credit in digital finance and its implications for corporate financial structures. The growing use of machine learning and big data analytics in credit assessment presents opportunities for enhancing trade credit efficiency, reducing default risks and improving supplier–buyer relationships (Liu and Wang, 2023). Additionally, policy interventions aimed at improving trade credit terms and protecting suppliers from delayed payments can contribute to a more resilient financial ecosystem. Given its complex impact, trade credit remains an indispensable component of corporate finance, requiring continuous assessment to ensure its sustainable and effective utilisation.

Trade credit also plays a significant role in capital structure decisions, influencing firms' financial leverage and working capital management (Molina and Preve, 2012). Firms that strategically use trade credit can optimise their debt–equity ratio, balancing short-term liquidity with long-term investment needs. Research suggests that firms experiencing growth, especially those with constrained access to bank credit, frequently rely on trade credit as an alternative financing channel to sustain expansion (Ferrando and Mulier, 2013). However, excessive reliance on trade credit can lead to an increase in financial risk, particularly for firms operating in sectors with high supplier dependency (Wilner, 2000; Cuñat, 2007). The trade-off between liquidity benefits and financial vulnerability remains a key consideration in corporate finance strategies.

As global supply chains continue to evolve, the integration of trade credit with alternative financing models, such as supply chain finance and reverse factoring, is becoming increasingly prevalent (Mateut, 2014). These mechanisms offer enhanced flexibility for both buyers and suppliers, allowing firms to optimise cash flow management while reducing financing costs. The growing emphasis on sustainability in corporate finance has also led to the development of green trade credit initiatives, promoting environmentally responsible business practices through supplier financing incentives (Bilyay-Erdogan and Öztürkkal, 2023).

In summary, trade credit plays a crucial role in corporate finance by providing liquidity, acting as a substitute for or complement to bank financing and serving as a monitoring mechanism; however, excessive reliance can pose financial risks. This discussion naturally leads to the next section, which examines short-term bank loans, another key source of corporate financing that differs from trade credit in terms of function, accessibility and classification criteria.

1.3 Short-term bank loans – function, availability, classification

Short-term bank loans play a significant role in corporate finance by providing firms with immediate liquidity to cover operational expenses, working capital requirements and unforeseen short-term obligations. Unlike long-term loans, which finance capital investments or business expansion, short-term bank loans are designed to bridge temporary cash flow gaps. These loans enable companies to maintain financial stability by ensuring the timely payment of suppliers, employee wages and tax obligations (Brealey, Myers and Allen, 2020).

One of the primary functions of short-term bank loans is their role as a liquidity management tool. Businesses often experience fluctuations in cash inflows and outflows due to seasonality, inventory cycles or delayed customer payments. Short-term loans provide the necessary flexibility to address these variations without disrupting business operations (Petersen and Rajan, 1997). In addition, these loans serve as a buffer against economic uncertainties, particularly for SMEs that might not have sufficient internal reserves to meet short-term financial challenges (Beck, Demirgüç-Kunt and Maksimovic, 2008).

Moreover, short-term bank loans can enhance firms' creditworthiness by establishing a strong borrowing history with financial institutions. Companies that demonstrate consistent repayment patterns may benefit from improved access to future financing opportunities, including lower interest rates and larger credit lines (Andrieu, Staglianò and van der Zwan, 2018). In this way, short-term bank loans act as a bridge for businesses aiming to acquire more substantial and longer-term financing.

The availability of short-term bank loans is influenced by a combination of firm-specific characteristics, financial institution policies and macroeconomic conditions, as summarised in Table 1.3. Factors such as creditworthiness, collateral and business performance are of key importance in determining whether a company qualifies for a short-term loan.

Financial institutions assess multiple firm-specific factors before granting short-term loans. Creditworthiness, measured through financial statements, payment histories and credit ratings, is a primary determinant of loan approval. Firms with strong credit histories and low debt ratios are more likely to receive favourable loan terms (Lawrenz and Oberndorfer, 2018).

Additionally, a company's financial leverage level plays a crucial role in credit decisions. Firms with high debt-to-equity ratios may face stricter lending conditions, as excessive leverage increases financial risk and limits creditworthiness and repayment capacity (Acharya, Almeida and Campello, 2013).

Lenders often require collateral to secure short-term loans, particularly for SMEs with limited credit histories. Fixed assets, inventory and accounts receivable are commonly used as collateral (Pinto *et al.*, 2023). The availability of tangible assets provides lenders with additional security, increasing the likelihood of loan approval.

Similarly, firms with higher cash reserves and strong liquidity ratios are perceived as lower-risk borrowers, increasing their chances for short-term credit (Białek-Jaworska and Nehrebecka, 2016). Banks' lending decisions are also influenced by business performance. Profitability metrics such as return on assets and total asset turnover might signal financial stability and therefore increase loan availability (Carvalho and Schiozer, 2015). Moreover, the quality of a firm's management can influence credit decisions, as banks are more likely to lend to businesses with experienced leadership and sound financial planning (Berger and Udell, 2006).

Table 1.3 Main factors affecting short-term loan availability

Character	*Factor*	*Description*
Internal	**Creditworthiness**	Firms with strong credit ratings have higher chances of loan approval.
	Collateral	Availability of tangible assets increases the likelihood of securing a loan.
	Liquidity position	Firms with higher cash reserves are perceived as lower-risk borrowers.
	Business performance	Profitability metrics influence banks' lending decisions.
	Leverage level	Firms with high existing debt may struggle to obtain additional financing due to higher default risk. Lenders evaluate debt-to-equity ratios and interest coverage ratios.
	Management quality	Experienced and reputable management teams are more likely to obtain loans due to their ability to ensure financial stability and strategic decision-making.
	Relationship with lenders	Long-standing relationships with financial institutions can facilitate access to credit, as trust and historical interactions reduce asymmetric information concerns.
External	**Bank lending policies**	Institutions' risk appetite and capital adequacy requirements impact loan availability.
	Macroeconomic conditions	Inflation, economic stability and monetary policies affect loan supply.
	Industry-specific risks	Riskier industries may face stricter lending conditions.
	Regulatory environment	Government-imposed regulations, capital requirements and financial stability policies affect bank lending behaviour and credit supply.
	Competition in the financial sector	A competitive banking sector with multiple lenders and alternative financing options (e.g., fintech lenders, credit unions) can increase short-term loan availability.
	Supply chain dependencies	Firms with strong supply chain dependencies may be riskier for lenders, particularly if key suppliers or customers face financial difficulties.

Sources: Own compilation based on: Biais and Gollier (1997); Boot (2000);Berger and Udell (2006); Beck, Demirgüç-Kunt and Maksimovic (2008); García-Teruel and Martínez-Solano (2010); Carbo-Valverde, Udell and Rodríguez-Fernández (2011);Acharya, Almeida and Campello (2013); Carvalho and Schiozer (2015); Białek-Jaworska and Nehrebecka (2016); Philippon (2016); Lawrenz and Oberndorfer (2018); Pinto, Henriques, Cardoso, *et al.* (2023).

Firm–bank relationships significantly influence loan accessibility, particularly for SMEs, which may face lending constraints despite financial stability (Bertrand and Murro, 2022; Pinto *et al.*, 2023). Studies indicate that firms with established banking relationships receive more favourable loan conditions, while those without sufficient collateral or credit history turn to trade credit (Hasan and Habib, 2019; Lefebvre, 2023).

Beyond firm-specific factors, external elements also impact the availability of short-term loans. Bank lending policies play a significant role in determining credit availability. Financial institutions adopt different risk appetites, which affect loan approval rates. Regulatory frameworks, capital adequacy requirements and risk management strategies determine banks' willingness to extend short-term credit (Beck, Demirgüç-Kunt and Maksimovic, 2008). In addition, firms with established banking relationships often benefit from more favourable lending terms. Long-term interactions with financial institutions can mitigate information asymmetry and lead to lower borrowing costs (Boot, 2000).

Macroeconomic conditions, such as inflation rates, economic stability and central bank monetary policies, also influence the availability of short-term loans. Periods of economic uncertainty often lead banks to tighten lending conditions, particularly for riskier borrowers (Carbo-Valverde, Udell and Rodríguez-Fernández, 2011). Moreover, the structure of the financial sector affects loan availability. A competitive banking environment with diverse lending institutions, including fintech firms and credit unions, can enhance access to short-term credit, particularly for SMEs (Philippon, 2016).

Different industries face varying levels of credit availability based on their risk profiles. For instance, manufacturing firms with tangible assets may find it easier to secure short-term loans compared to service-based firms with fewer collateral options (García-Teruel and Martínez-Solano, 2010). Additionally, supply chain dependencies may influence loan approval, as firms highly reliant on specific suppliers or customers may be perceived as riskier borrowers due to potential disruptions in cash flows (Biais and Gollier, 1997).

Short-term bank loans can be classified into different categories based on their structure, repayment terms and purpose. Overdraft facilities provide businesses with the flexibility to withdraw funds exceeding their account balance, up to a pre-approved limit. These facilities are typically unsecured and carry variable interest rates, making them an attractive option for firms facing short-term cash shortages (Afrifa *et al.*, 2023). However, overdrafts can be expensive due to higher interest rates and fees associated with exceeding credit limits (Opler *et al.*, 1999).

A revolving credit line functions as a reusable credit facility, allowing firms to borrow and repay funds multiple times within a specified period. Unlike overdrafts, revolving credit lines are typically secured and may involve fixed borrowing limits. They offer flexibility in managing working capital but require businesses to meet regular interest payments (Brealey, Myers and Allen, 2020). Short-term loans involve borrowing a fixed amount of capital with a predetermined repayment schedule. These loans are usually secured against business assets and carry fixed or variable interest rates. They are appropriate for financing specific short-term projects or covering seasonal expenses (Petersen and Rajan, 1997).

Bridge loans are temporary financing solutions designed to 'bridge' the gap between immediate financial needs and long-term funding sources. These loans are commonly used in merger and acquisition transactions or when awaiting permanent financing approval (Diamond, 1991). Although bridge loans offer rapid access to funds, they typically carry high interest rates due to their short duration and risk level.

Another short-term financial instruments, i.e., invoice discounting and factoring allow firms to convert outstanding receivables into immediate cash. In invoice discounting, businesses receive funds from a lender based on a percentage of their invoices, whereas factoring involves selling invoices to a financial institution at a discount (Mian and Smith Jr., 1992). These financing methods provide quick liquidity but reduce the overall receivable amount.

In summary, short-term bank loans are indispensable in corporate finance, offering businesses the liquidity needed to sustain daily operations, manage cash flow fluctuations and capitalise on short-term opportunities. Their availability depends on firm-specific characteristics, institutional policies and macroeconomic conditions. The various classifications of short-term bank loans cater to different financial needs, ranging from flexible overdrafts to structured term loans and alternative solutions like factoring. By understanding the role and classification of these loans, businesses can make informed financing decisions that align with their strategic goals and financial liquidity management.

1.4 Substitution and complementarity between trade credit and bank loans

Trade credit and bank loans are two primary sources of short-term financing for firms, but their relationship varies across businesses, industries and macroeconomic conditions. This relationship may be characterised as substitutive, complementary, or context dependent, a distinction that bears significant implications for financial management and policy formulation. Whether trade credit and bank credit act as substitutes or complements depends, among others, on the availability of credit, firm-specific characteristics and economic circumstances.

The substitution effect occurs when firms use one financing source as a replacement for the other. In this case, an increase in trade credit usage coincides with a decrease in bank loan utilisation and vice versa. The substitution effect is often observed in cases where bank credit is scarce, costly or inaccessible, as first reported by Meltzer (1960). Firms facing bank lending constraints, whether due to weak creditworthiness, high interest rates or macroeconomic downturns, may turn to suppliers for financing. Suppliers often have more flexible lending criteria and better information about a firm's financial health through repeated transactions, making trade credit a worthwhile alternative (Petersen and Rajan, 1997; Palacín-Sánchez, Canto-Cuevas and Di-Pietro, 2019).

In contrast, as theorised by Biais and Gollier (1997), the complementarity effect suggests that firms use trade credit and bank loans simultaneously to optimise their financial structure. Instead of replacing one another, trade credit and bank loans work together to provide liquidity and financial flexibility. Firms that have strong banking relationships may still use trade credit as an additional financing channel to extend payment periods and manage cash flows more efficiently. This effect is often seen in firms with established supplier relationships and stable access to banking services, allowing them to benefit from multiple financing sources (Afrifa *et al.*, 2023; Tsuruta, 2023). Theoretical frameworks suggest that trade credit and bank loans can complement each other due to their differing advantages. Bank loans provide structured financing with lower costs in stable financial environments, whereas trade credit offers flexibility and informal arrangements that can support firms in liquidity constraints (Biais and Gollier, 1997; Nilsen, 2002; Yang, 2011).

Empirical studies provide mixed evidence on the substitution and complementarity effects of trade credit and bank loans. The prevalence of one effect over the other depends on firm-specific, industry-specific and macroeconomic factors. Some studies confirm that trade credit acts as a substitute for bank loans, particularly in financially constrained firms or during periods of economic instability. The credit rationing hypothesis suggests that smaller firms, which often lack access to bank loans due to their higher default risk, turn to trade credit as an alternative source of financing (Petersen and Rajan, 1997; Palacín-Sánchez, Canto-Cuevas and Di-Pietro, 2019). During the 2008 financial crisis, many firms faced restricted access to bank credit, leading to increased reliance on supplier credit (Casey and O'Toole, 2014; Bussoli and Marino, 2018; Tsuruta, 2023). Firms in high-risk industries or developing economies also exhibit a stronger substitution effect due to limited access to banking services (Andrieu, Staglianò and van der Zwan, 2018). Table 1.4 provides a summary of empirical studies which report a negative relationship between trade credit and bank credit, that is, which support the substitution hypothesis.

On the other hand, some studies highlight situations where trade credit and bank loans complement each other. Liquidity management strategies suggest that firms use trade credit alongside bank loans to extend their working capital cycles and ensure financial flexibility (Afrifa *et al.*, 2023; Tsuruta, 2023). The signalling effect explains that firms using both trade credit and bank loans demonstrate financial stability and creditworthiness, enhancing their access to future financing (Agostino and Trivieri, 2014). Petersen and Rajan (1997) argue that the use of trade credit can serve as a signal of firm quality. Firms that secure both bank loans and trade credit tend to be perceived as financially stable and creditworthy. This dual usage suggests that such firms not only have access to traditional financing but also rely on trade credit as an alternative source, thereby enhancing their reputation and access to future financing.

Firms with strong banking relationships often negotiate favourable trade credit terms, suggesting that the two financing sources are not mutually exclusive but instead support one another. Ng, Smith and Smith (1999) provide evidence consistent with this view. Their analysis of interfirm credit terms demonstrates that firms with strong banking relationships tend to secure more favourable trade credit terms from their suppliers. This finding suggests that robust bank relationships enhance a firm's overall creditworthiness and bargaining

Table 1.4 Summary of some empirical evidence on the negative relationship between trade credit and bank loan: substitution hypothesis

Study	*Context*
Meltzer (1960)	Tightened money market conditions
Schwartz (1974)	A stylised economic model to illustrate the conditions under which trade credit serves as a mechanism to overcome financing constraints
Biais and Gollier (1997)	Relationships with banks, information asymmetries, periods of monetary tightening
Petersen and Rajan (1997)	US small firms with limited access to capital markets
Deloof and Jegers (1999)	Belgian firms engaged in intragroup transactions; product quality and group-specific factors
Kohler, Britton and Yates (2000)	UK quoted companies during recession
Nilsen (2002)	US manufacturing firms of varying sizes; credit-constrained environments, periods of monetary contraction
Burkart and Ellingsen (2004)	Theoretical model, adverse selection and collateral issues
Cull, Xu and Zhu (2009)	Industrial firms in China
García-Teruel and Martínez-Solano (2010)	SME from seven European countries, homogeneity in the factors determining trade credit
Hui, Xiaojun and Shunming (2011)	China; counter-cyclical behaviour of the substitution
Kling, Salima and Eleimon (2011)	Publicly listed non-financial firms
Molina and Preve (2009)	US firms in financial distress
Bastos and Pindado (2013)	Firms from Argentina, Brazil and Turkey, financial crisis
Garcia-Appendini and Montoriol-Garriga (2013)	Spanish non-financial firms during the crisis period when bank lending was severely constrained
Ogawa, Sterken and Tokutsu (2013)	Japanese small firms
Casey and O'Toole (2014)	Euro area SMEs facing credit rationing, financial crises
Engemann, Eck and Schnitzer (2014)	German manufacturing firms, internationally active
McGuinness and Hogan (2014)	Irish SMEs in the aftermath of the financial crisis of 2008

(*Continued*)

Table 1.4 (Continued)

Study	*Context*
Lawrenz and Oberndorfer (2018)	SMEs and large firms in Germany; strengthened substitution effect during the crisis among large firms, but not among SMEs
Levine, Lin and Xie (2018)	34 countries, systemic banking crises, economies with higher levels of social trust
Palacín-Sánchez, Canto-Cuevas and Di-Pietro (2019)	SMEs from 12 European Union, institutional factors
Duliniec and Świda (2021)	Polish listed companies
Wang *et al.* (2021)	SMEs across 19 EU countries, economic stability vs. downturns
Pinto, Henriques, Cardoso, *et al.* (2023)	Portuguese SMEs, financial crisis

Source: Own elaboration based on the listed literature items.

power, enabling it to negotiate better trade credit conditions. In other words, rather than acting as mutually exclusive sources of finance, bank credit and trade credit can strengthen each other (Agostino and Trivieri, 2014). Table 1.5 presents a summary of empirical studies supporting the complementarity hypothesis between trade credit and bank loans, that is a positive relationship.

The mixed evidence on the relationship between trade credit and bank loans indicates that it might be influenced by other factors. Firm size plays a crucial role, as smaller businesses are more likely to experience substitution effects due to restricted access to bank financing, whereas larger firms often integrate both sources for efficient capital management (Petersen and Rajan, 1997; Palacín-Sánchez, Canto-Cuevas and Di-Pietro, 2019).

Industry characteristics also shape financing decisions; capital-intensive industries tend to rely more on bank loans, while trade-dependent sectors may make greater use of trade credit. Beck, Demirgüç-Kunt and Maksimovic (2008) provide evidence that industry characteristics significantly influence firms' financing decisions. Their analysis shows that capital-intensive industries – characterised by high asset tangibility – tend to have easier access to bank loans, while sectors that are more dependent on trade (and often

Table 1.5 Summary of empirical evidence on the positive relationship between trade credit bank loan: complementarity hypothesis

Study	*Context*
McMillan and Woodruff (1999)	Private firms in Vietnam, relational contracting factors as determinants of trade credit
Demirguc-Kunt and Maksimovic (2001)	Firm-level data from 39 countries, country's banking system and legal infrastructure as predictors of trade credit
Ono (2001)	Japanese manufacturing companies, monetary policy
Fisman and Raturi (2004)	Five African countries, monopoly power vs. credit provision
Cuñat (2007)	UK manufacturing firms, retailers and wholesalers
Beck, Demirgüç-Kunt and Maksimovic (2008)	Firm-level surveys from both developed and developing countries across different industries; firm size effect and cross-country heterogeneity
Uesugi and Yamashiro (2008)	Small Japanese businesses
Cole (2010)	Small US firms
Alarcón (2011)	Spanish agrofood industry
Vaidya (2011)	Indian manufacturing firms
Santos and Silva (2014)	Portuguese industrial companies
Carvalho and Schiozer (2015)	Survey of micro and SMEs in Brazil
Deloof and La Rocca (2015)	Italian SMEs; local financial development and trade credit in an integrated financial market
Psillaki and Eleftheriou (2015)	French SMEs from four industries
Andrieu, Staglianò and van der Zwan (2018)	European SMEs, industry and country factors
Maksimovic and Frank (2005)	While adverse selection pressures can push firms to substitute trade credit for bank credit, the equilibrium also accommodates situations where trade credit is used in conjunction with other forms of financing.
Marotta (2005)	Italian manufacturing firms: discount proposals effectively reduce payment delays mainly for export-oriented customers, whereas for domestic transactions their role is ambiguous
Taketa and Udell (2007)	SMEs in Japan during the financial crisis period
Love and Zaidi (2010)	SMEs in four East Asian countries before and after the financial crisis of 1998

(*Continued*)

Table 1.5 (Continued)

Study	*Context*
Agostino and Trivieri (2014)	microdata of Italian SMEs; signalling effect particularly pronounced during the early stages of bank–firm relationships
Yazdanfar and Öhman (2017)	Swedish SMEs
Andrieu, Staglianò and van der Zwan (2018)	Survey data on European SMEs
Ma and Ma (2020)	Privately (i.e., non-state) controlled but publicly listed firms in China

Source: Own elaboration based on the listed literature items.

have lower tangible collateral) rely more heavily on trade credit. This finding suggests that the two financing sources are not mutually exclusive; instead, industry-specific factors drive the relative reliance on bank credit versus trade credit.

The country-specific financial environment further determines the relationship between trade credit and bank loans. Firms operating in volatile markets often balance both financing options to mitigate risk. Beck, Demirgüç-Kunt and Maksimovic (2008) show that in markets characterised by uncertainty, firms tend to diversify their financing sources, rather than rely exclusively on one type of financing. Moreover, developed economies with strong banking infrastructure tend to exhibit complementarity (Demirguc-Kunt and Maksimovic, 2001), whereas developing economies, where access to bank financing is more limited, show stronger substitution effects (Casey and O'Toole, 2014).

Macroeconomic conditions also play a significant role in shaping financing decisions. During economic downturns, firms rely more on trade credit as banks tighten lending conditions, reinforcing the substitution effect (Nilsen, 2002; Bastos and Pindado, 2013). In stable financial periods, firms are more likely to leverage both financing sources simultaneously (Maksimovic and Frank, 2005).

Firms with established banking relationships generally exhibit complementarity effects, using trade credit to supplement liquidity while maintaining access to bank loans (Psillaki and Eleftheriou, 2015; Norden, Van Kampen and Illueca, 2021). Young firms or those operating in high-risk industries are more likely to substitute bank loans with trade credit due to restricted borrowing options (Cole, 2010).

The relationship between trade credit and bank loans is complex and varies based on firm, industry and macroeconomic factors. While some firms substitute trade credit for bank loans due to credit constraints, others leverage both financing sources to optimise liquidity. As shown in Table 1.6, many empirical studies provide mixed evidence on the relationship between trade credit and bank loans, indicating that firms may use these financing sources either as substitutes or complements depending on various factors.

These mixed findings emphasise the importance of factors such as firm size, financial constraints, industry-specific conditions and macroeconomic environments, which shape the trade credit-bank loan relationship and make it context-dependent.

1.5 Determinants of corporate short-term financing behaviour: from firm characteristics to industry and country contexts

Corporate short-term financing decisions are shaped by a range of internal and external factors. This section outlines key influences, including firm-specific attributes, firm size, industry characteristics and country-level institutional and macroeconomic conditions.

Firm-specific factors play an essential role in shaping corporate short-term financing policies, particularly regarding the amount of trade credit obtained and provided. Trade credit serves as both an alternative and a complement to bank credit and its utilisation is influenced by a wide array of firm-level characteristics that affect a company's creditworthiness, bargaining power and liquidity management strategies. Apart from short-term bank loans, several other firm-specific variables – such as collateral, inventory levels, cash holdings, cost structures, leverage, profitability and asset efficiency – significantly determine how firms manage trade credit. The theoretical background and empirical evidence regarding these firm-specific determinants are synthesised in Table 1.7, which summarises their predicted and observed relationships with trade credit practices.

Overall, firm-specific characteristics significantly influence corporate short-term financing decisions, although – as demonstrated in the above literature review – their impact is highly context-dependent.

Table 1.6 Summary of empirical studies providing mixed evidence on the relationship between trade credit bank loan: substitution or complementarity hypotheses

Study	*Context*
Cunningham (2005)	Canadian firms, substitution for medium wealth firms (i.e. firms whose investment is less likely to be constrained by availability of external funds), complementarity for low wealth firms (i.e. firms whose investments are more likely to be finance constrained)
Maksimovic and Frank (2005)	While adverse selection pressures can push firms to substitute trade credit for bank credit, the equilibrium also accommodates situations where trade credit is used in conjunction with other forms of financing.
Marotta (2005)	Italian manufacturing firms: discount proposals effectively reduce payment delays mainly for export-oriented customers, whereas for domestic transactions their role is ambiguous
(Fukuda, Kasuya and Akashi, 2006)	SMEs in Japan during the banking crisis, substitution during non-crisis period, complementarity during the crisis
Bougheas, Mateut and Mizen (2009)	Quoted and unquoted UK firms; while bank loans enable higher production (complementing trade credit on the asset side), they also serve as a substitute for delaying payments (reducing trade credit on the liability side)
Norden, Van Kampen and Illueca (2021)	SMEs from the five largest European countries; low-credit quality (i.e. high-risk) SMEs tend to substitute bank credit for trade credit more than high-credit quality firms
Yang (2011b)	US-listed manufacturing firms: substitution in tight monetary periods, complementarity for looser monetary episodes
Cai, Chen and Xiao (2014)	China: substitution if the retailer's internal capital grows, complementarity if the retailer's internal capital is substantially low
Lin and Chou (2015)	China: substitution for the demand of trade credit (i.e., accounts payable), complementarity for the supply of trade credit (i.e., accounts receivable); firm size effect
Białek-Jaworska and Nehrebecka (2016)	Polish companies: substitution for small companies, complementarity for medium size and large companies
Canto-Cuevas, Palacín-Sánchez and di Pietro (2016)	Spanish manufacturing SMEs, a quantile regression approach: complementarity for large and mature firms, substitution for small, young and financially constrained companies

Table 1.6 (Continued)

Study	*Context*
Norden, Van Kampen and Illueca (2021)	SMEs from France, Germany, Italy, Spain and the UK; substitution and complementary relation are almost equally likely during no crisis period, whereas complementarity dominates during crisis
Afrifa *et al.* (2023)	UK public and private firms: substitution for public firms with easy access to external finance, complementarity for private firms with limited access to financial markets

Source: Own elaboration based on the listed literature items.

A key firm-specific factor warranting separate consideration is **firm size**, which significantly shapes short-term financing behaviour; its effect and moderating influence are discussed next. Firm size influences access to credit, financing preferences and strategic liquidity management. Theoretical frameworks such as the pecking order theory suggest that smaller firms are more reliant on external sources like trade credit when internal resources are insufficient (Myers and Majluf, 1984). This reliance stems from pervasive credit rationing faced by SMEs, which are often constrained in the formal financial sector (García-Teruel and Martínez-Solano, 2010; Palacín-Sánchez, Canto-Cuevas and Di-Pietro, 2019). In contrast, larger firms enjoy economies of scale and greater flexibility in selecting financing instruments (Demirgüç-Kunt and Maksimovic, 2001).

Access to bank credit and trade credit is shaped by firm size through mechanisms such as asymmetric information, risk perception and financial transparency. SMEs tend to face more stringent borrowing conditions, including higher interest rates and stricter collateral requirements, while large firms benefit from more favourable terms (Petersen and Rajan, 1997; Beck, Demirgüç-Kunt and Maksimovic, 2008). Credit rationing theory (Stiglitz and Weiss, 1981) states that adverse selection results in lending constraints for riskier, smaller borrowers. Empirical studies confirm this: SMEs experience higher borrowing costs and greater reliance on alternative funding sources, such as trade credit (Berger and Udell, 2006; Carbó-Valverde, Rodríguez-Fernández and Udell, 2016).

Table 1.7 Summary of theoretical predictions and empirical findings on firm-specific determinants of trade credit

Factor and its relationship with trade credit		*Theory, explanation*	*Empirical evidence*
Collateral	+	Collateral as an indicator of creditworthiness reduces information asymmetry between firms and suppliers (Ross, 1977; Tirole, 2006). A firm with substantial tangible assets signals financial solidity, which may encourage suppliers to extend trade credit on favourable terms (signalling theory).	Lawrenz and Oberndorfer (2018) report that high collateral increases suppliers' willingness to grant credit in contexts with significant information asymmetry.
	-	High collateral improves access to bank loans, reducing reliance on supplier credit (debt capacity hypothesis: Shleifer and Vishny, 1992). Firms with substantial collateral may prefer bank financing over trade credit due to more favourable conditions.	Pinto *et al.* (2023) find that firms with higher collateral obtain less trade credit, consistent with substitution between supplier credit and bank loans.
Inventory	+	High inventory signals operational preparedness and continuity, which may improve supplier confidence and facilitate credit granted to customers (working capital theory: Lin and Chou, 2015; signalling theory: Ross, 1977; Tirole, 2006). Inventory may also serve as collateral to secure credit.	Lin and Chou (2015) and Białek-Jaworska and Nehrebecka (2016) show that firms with higher inventory holdings tend to use more supplier credit and, in some contexts, grant more trade credit.

Table 1.7 (Continued)

Factor and its relationship with trade credit	*Theory, explanation*	*Empirical evidence*
	- High inventory may strain liquidity or signal inefficiency or obsolescence risk (signalling theory: Ross, 1977), which can reduce suppliers' willingness to extend credit and discourage firms from granting credit to preserve cash.	Yang and Birge (2017) find that firms with high inventories rely more on supplier credit but are cautious in granting credit to customers.
Cash holdings	+ Cash reserves signal financial stability and reduce perceived credit risk (signalling theory: Myers and Majluf, 1984), encouraging suppliers to offer favourable credit terms and enabling firms to grant trade credit strategically.	Petersen and Rajan (1997), Martínez-Sola, García-Teruel and Martínez-Solano (2014) and McGuinness, Hogan and Powell (2018) show that cash-rich firms are more willing to grant trade credit as part of a competitive strategy.
	- High cash reserves reduce liquidity constraints and lessen dependence on supplier credit (liquidity management theory: Fazzari and Petersen, 1993; substitution hypothesis). Firms may prefer to use internal funds rather than external short-term credit.	Martinez-Sola, García-Teruel and Martinez-Solano (2012) and Fazzari, Hubbard and Petersen (1988) report that firms with more liquidity obtain less trade credit; Laghari and Chengang (2019) and Harris, Roark and Li (2019) confirm that liquidity buffers reduce the need for trade credit but do not eliminate reliance on it.
Cost of goods sold	+ A high COGS ratio reduces profit margins and increases liquidity pressures, leading firms to rely on supplier credit to bridge working capital gaps (working capital management theory: Petersen and Rajan (1997); pecking order theory: Myers and Majluf, 1984).	Lin and Chou (2015), Deloof and Jegers (1999), Hoang, Xiao and Akbar (2019) and Shi, Wang and Tan (2020) find that firms with high production costs tend to rely more heavily on trade credit obtained.

(*Continued*)

Table 1.7 (Continued)

Factor and its relationship with trade credit		*Theory, explanation*	*Empirical evidence*
	-	High COGS may signal financial fragility (signalling theory: Ross, 1977; Biais and Gollier, 1997), prompting suppliers to tighten credit terms and discouraging firms from extending credit due to constrained liquidity.	García-Appendini and Montoriol-Garriga (2013) and McGuinness, Hogan and Powell (2018) observe that firms under cost pressure are less likely to offer trade credit to customers.
Leverage	+	Highly leveraged firms may substitute supplier credit for constrained bank loans (financial constraint hypothesis: Petersen and Rajan (1997). Trade credit can function as an alternative financing channel when access to bank credit is limited.	Cuñat (2007) and Carvalho and Schiozer (2015) show that leveraged firms are more dependent on trade credit, especially when credit constraints exist in the banking market.
	-	High leverage increases perceived credit risk, which may lead suppliers to ration credit and constrain firms' ability to offer trade credit (credit risk hypothesis; Lawrenz and Oberndorfer, 2018).	García-Teruel and Martínez-Solano (2010), Lawrenz and Oberndorfer (2018) and McGuinness, Hogan and Powell (2018) report that suppliers limit credit to highly leveraged firms and that such firms also grant less credit to customers.
Profitability	+	High profitability improves liquidity and allows firms to strategically grant credit to support sales growth, foster customer relationships and enhance competitiveness (strategic financing hypothesis; signalling theory: Ross, 1977; Myers and Majluf, 1984).	Martínez-Sola, García-Teruel and Martínez-Solano (2014), McGuinness, Hogan and Powell (2018) and Agostino and Trivieri (2014) demonstrate that profitable firms are more active in granting trade credit as part of business strategy.

Table 1.7 (Continued)

Factor and its relationship with trade credit		*Theory, explanation*	*Empirical evidence*
	-	Low profitability constrains access to external financing, increasing reliance on trade credit obtained from suppliers (financial constraint hypothesis; pecking order theory: Myers and Majluf, 1984).	Yazdanfar and Öhman (2016) and Molina and Preve (2012) provide evidence that less profitable firms use more supplier credit due to financial constraints.
Operational efficiency	+	Firms with high asset turnover generate cash more quickly, enabling them to offer credit to customers as a strategic tool to build customer loyalty and market share (signalling theory: Ross, 1977; strategic financing hypothesis).	Lin and Chou (2015) and García-Teruel and Martínez-Solano (2010) report that operationally efficient firms are more likely to extend credit to customers as part of sales strategy.
	-	High operational efficiency reduces reliance on supplier credit by ensuring strong internal cash flow (efficiency hypothesis: Lin and Chou, 2015).	Lin and Chou (2015) and García-Teruel and Martínez-Solano (2010) observe that efficient firms rely less on trade credit obtained from suppliers.

Source: Own elaboration based on the listed literature items.

Trade credit obtained and extended is also affected by firm size. Larger firms tend to extend more trade credit to smaller buyers, leveraging their stronger financial positions and bargaining power (Petersen and Rajan, 1997; McMillan and Woodruff, 1999). SMEs often depend on supplier credit, particularly during periods of tight bank lending (García-Appendini and Montoriol-Garriga, 2013). According to the substitution hypothesis, trade credit serves as an alternative to institutional credit for financially constrained firms (Petersen and Rajan, 1997). In contrast, the complementarity hypothesis suggests that firms with better access to bank loans may also receive more trade credit, as suppliers use banking relationships as proxies for financial health (Love, Preve and Sarria-Allende, 2007; Ferrando and Mulier, 2013).

The pecking order theory also explains financing preferences linked to firm size: SMEs prefer internal funds, followed by trade credit and resort to external debt only when other options are exhausted (Myers and Majluf, 1984). SMEs frequently rely on trade credit to fund working capital, often before approaching banks (García-Teruel and Martínez-Solano, 2010). Peel, Wilson and Howorth (2000) observe that SMEs may also provide trade credit to attract and retain customers, despite the risks and financial strain it imposes.

Conversely, large firms prefer external financing due to their strong credit ratings and lower perceived risk. Palacín-Sánchez, Canto-Cuevas and Di-Pietro (2019) find that SMEs exhibit a simultaneous dependence on both trade and bank credit, though they rely more heavily on trade credit when constrained. Institutional factors, such as legal system efficiency and financial development, further influence this dynamic, making financing decisions context-dependent.

Bargaining power, closely linked to firm size, significantly affects financing outcomes. Larger firms can negotiate lower loan rates and extended repayment terms, while SMEs face stricter conditions and shorter maturities (Mian and Smith, 1992); Petersen and Rajan, 1997). Chodorow-Reich *et al.* (2022) report that smaller firms pay higher interest rates, offer more collateral and often deal with expiring credit lines. Ghulam, Hakro and Naumani (2025) confirm that SMEs face higher rejection rates for trade credit, increasing their reliance on more expensive financing options.

Larger firms also act as financial intermediaries, strategically using trade credit to manage liquidity and enhance customer relationships (Cuñat, 2007). Bougheas, Mateut and Mizen (2009) note that SMEs, constrained by credit terms and weak bargaining positions, struggle to optimise working capital in the same way.

Short-term bank financing instruments also differ by firm size. While large firms access overdrafts, revolving credit lines and commercial paper, SMEs are more reliant on standard bank loans with rigid terms (Caglio, Darst and Kalemli-Özcan, 2021). SMEs also turn more frequently to informal sources like internal funds or personal networks (Gur *et al.*, 2023). The OECD (2024) reports that SMEs face higher financing costs, amplified by risk-based pricing models and reduced loan approvals during periods of rising interest rates.

In trade credit relationships, firm size again plays a decisive role. SMEs depend heavily on supplier credit but face stricter terms due to default risk and limited bargaining power (Lawrenz and Oberndorfer,

2018). Large firms, by contrast, provide extended payment terms to customers, leveraging their financial flexibility and robust credit profiles. Ng, Smith and Smith (1999) show that firms with strong bank relationships are more likely to extend favourable credit terms, supporting their role as liquidity providers in supply chains.

The influence of macroeconomic conditions and market disruptions also varies by firm size. During financial crises or credit tightening, SMEs suffer disproportionately from reduced bank lending, pushing them towards greater trade credit reliance (Carbo-Valverde, Udell and Rodríguez-Fernández, 2011; Casey and O'Toole, 2014). Larger firms remain more resilient, adapting their financing mix to maintain liquidity (Nilsen, 2002; Carbó-Valverde, Rodríguez-Fernández and Udell, 2016).

In sum, firm size fundamentally shapes access to and composition of short-term financing. SMEs typically face tighter credit conditions, reduced negotiating power and greater reliance on trade credit. Large firms benefit from scale economies, diversified funding options and favourable borrowing terms. Understanding these firm-size effects is essential for analysing short-term financing decisions under varying institutional and macroeconomic conditions.

While firm size remains a significant factor in shaping short-term financing behaviour, these decisions are also closely tied to the broader **industrial context** in which firms operate. Industry-specific characteristics – such as asset structures, revenue stability, risk profiles and supply chain dynamics – create distinct financial environments that influence the extent to which firms rely on bank credit or trade credit for working capital management.

Capital-intensive industries, such as manufacturing and construction, typically benefit from easier access to short-term bank loans due to their abundant tangible assets that can serve as collateral (Rajan and Zingales, 1995; Frank and Goyal, 2009). Asset-backed lending dominates in these sectors because banks perceive machinery, equipment and real estate as reliable safeguards against default risk (Mateut, Bougheas and Mizen, 2006). In contrast, service-based sectors like software or consulting – characterised by fewer tangible assets – tend to rely more heavily on trade credit or internal liquidity to meet their working capital needs (Beck, Demirgüç-Kunt and Maksimovic, 2008).

The redeployability of assets within an industry further shapes financing patterns. Firms operating in sectors where fixed assets are highly specialised and difficult to repurpose tend to exhibit greater dependence on trade credit (Hasan and Alam, 2022). Asset specificity thereby functions as a constraint on bank-based finance, particularly for firms facing external credit restrictions.

Industry-related cash flow volatility also affects short-term financing strategies. Firms in seasonal or cyclical industries – such as retail, hospitality and tourism – must manage uneven revenue streams, leading them to adopt more flexible financing approaches. During off-peak periods, such firms often turn to trade credit, which provides deferred payment options aligned with short-term liquidity needs (Cuñat, 2007; García-Appendini and Montoriol-Garriga, 2013). Conversely, firms in stable industries like utilities or pharmaceuticals benefit from predictable cash flows and thus secure more favourable credit terms from both banks and suppliers (Danielson and Scott, 2004).

Risk exposure at the industry level is another significant determinant. High-risk sectors – such as construction, early-stage technology, or mining – face stricter lending standards from financial institutions due to long investment cycles and susceptibility to macroeconomic shocks (Bărbuţă-Mişu, 2018; Chod, Lyandres and Yang, 2019). In such settings, suppliers often step in as alternative lenders, leveraging superior knowledge of sector-specific risks. Meanwhile, firms in more stable industries typically benefit from better loan conditions, including longer maturities and lower interest rates (Avalos, Doerr and Pinter, 2025).

Empirical studies confirm these sectoral disparities. Manufacturing firms, with their asset-rich profiles and relatively predictable revenues, often enjoy greater access to institutional short-term credit compared to those in service or retail sectors (Angori and Aristei, 2022; Castaldo *et al.*, 2023). In contrast, regulatory oversight and higher compliance costs in certain sectors can lead to increased borrowing costs and reduced credit availability (Trebbi and Zhang, 2022; Akang, 2023).

The availability and use of trade credit also differ significantly across industries. Firms with long production cycles or significant inventory requirements – such as wholesalers and manufacturers – commonly rely on supplier credit to bridge financing gaps (Barrot, 2016; Tingbani *et al.*, 2024). Retail and service industries, which often operate with faster cash conversion cycles, are less dependent on trade credit, as immediate liquidity generation reduces the need for deferred payment structures. Suppliers in capital-intensive industries are also more likely to offer trade credit in support of long-standing commercial relationships.

The practice of extending trade credit similarly reflects industry norms. Firms in stable sectors with strong bargaining positions often grant generous payment terms to their customers, using trade credit as a competitive tool to strengthen long-term relationships (Ng, Smith and Smith, 1999; Lehar, Song and Yuan, 2020). In contrast, firms in sectors characterised by rapid turnover or perishable goods – such as food retail or hospitality – tend to offer shorter repayment windows due to their own liquidity constraints.

Trade credit and bank loans may act as either substitutes or complements depending on the sector. In high-risk or bank-constrained industries, trade credit often substitutes for limited formal financing, particularly during periods of tightened credit conditions (Machokoto, Gyimah and Ibrahim, 2022). During economic downturns, this substitutive function becomes more pronounced, as firms in affected industries increase their reliance on supplier credit to sustain operations (Jou, Li and Wang, 2024). Conversely, in capital-intensive sectors, bank loans and trade credit are often used in tandem to optimise liquidity and allocate financial resources efficiently across different operational functions (Love, Preve and Sarria-Allende, 2007; Ferrando and Mulier, 2013).

Credit allocation within industries is also influenced by institutional frameworks and regulatory environments. Regulatory burdens in certain sectors may increase financing costs, particularly for firms that operate under complex compliance regimes. Moreover, banks' risk assessment models account for sector-specific factors, resulting in industry-based segmentation of credit markets (Carbó-Valverde, Rodríguez-Fernández and Udell, 2016; Ma and Fang, 2023). This segmentation has practical implications for short-term financing strategies, highlighting disparities in liquidity access across industries.

Ultimately, industry-specific characteristics significantly affect the structure, availability and terms of short-term financing. Firms in capital-intensive, stable and asset-rich industries benefit from favourable access to bank loans and supplier credit, while firms in volatile, intangible-intensive or high-risk sectors often confront constraints that push them towards alternative financing options. Recognising the influence of industry context on short-term finance is essential for designing liquidity strategies that align with sector-specific risks and opportunities. These differences highlight the necessity of incorporating industry-specific factors into corporate financial planning, especially in managing short-term funding under varying economic and institutional environments.

While industry-specific characteristics shape corporate short-term financing behaviour through structural, operational and sectoral factors, these patterns are further conditioned by the broader national environment in which firms operate. Differences in legal systems, institutional quality, macroeconomic conditions and cultural norms exert a substantial influence on how financing decisions are made. Thus, to fully understand the variation in trade credit and short-term bank loan usage, it is essential to consider the **country effect**, which introduces systemic variation beyond firm and industry levels.

The country context plays a critical role in shaping corporate short-term financing strategies, complementing firm- and industry-level determinants. Legal and institutional frameworks are crucial to this effect. Strong creditor protection, efficient contract enforcement and robust bankruptcy laws enhance access to trade credit and bank loans by reducing default risk and increasing suppliers' willingness to extend credit (La Porta *et al.*, 1997, 1998; Sautner and Vladimirov, 2018). Conversely, weak legal systems create uncertainty, elevate transaction costs and constrain access to external finance, especially for SMEs (Claessens and Klapper, 2005; Moro, Maresch and Ferrando, 2018).

Macroeconomic conditions also affect credit practices. High inflation, exchange rate volatility and fiscal instability reduce firms' ability to use and extend trade credit (Demirgüç-Kunt and Maksimovic, 2001; Wang *et al.*, 2021). In contrast, stable financial systems provide more predictable financing conditions, enabling firms to substitute trade credit with institutional credit (Andrieu, Staglianò and van der Zwan, 2018). In developing markets with underdeveloped financial systems, trade credit often fills institutional credit gaps, albeit inadequately (Beck, Demirgüç-Kunt and Maksimovic, 2008).

Cultural norms further influence credit behaviour. Dimensions such as uncertainty avoidance and collectivism shape trust, negotiation styles and tolerance for payment delays (Hofstede, 2001; Belghitar and Mateus, 2016). High uncertainty avoidance cultures may encourage stricter credit terms, while collectivist societies rely more on informal, trust-based arrangements (Hoang *et al.*, 2023; Ziętek-Kwaśniewska, 2023).

Regulatory and tax frameworks also shape credit incentives. Jurisdictions with favourable tax treatment for bad debts or clear receivables valuation practices support greater trade credit use (Pindado and Bastos, 2009; Zhao, Tang and Wang, 2025). Moreover, enforcement inefficiencies, as shown by Aguiar-Díaz, Mruk and Ruiz-Mallorquí (2024), elevate systemic risk by increasing receivable defaults.

The structure of national economies matters as well. Manufacturing-heavy countries often exhibit higher trade credit dependence due to longer production cycles and inventory needs, while service-oriented economies rely less on supplier credit (Ge and Qiu, 2007; Canto-Cuevas, Palacín-Sánchez and Di Pietro, 2019). State ownership in banking can further distort access to institutional credit, encouraging trade credit reliance (Yeyati *et al.*, 2007).

Credit infrastructure and public policy play a moderating role. Well-functioning registries and credit guarantee schemes reduce information asymmetries and facilitate interfirm financing, particularly for SMEs (Kaya, 2024). Supranational policies, such as the EU's Late Payment Directive, aim to harmonise credit practices but are unevenly enforced across member states (Lefebvre, 2023; Gongeta, 2024).

For multinational corporations (MNCs), the country effect necessitates decentralised credit management to adapt to local regulatory and cultural conditions (Grant and Venzin, 2009). In contrast, SMEs face greater challenges, often relying on informal networks and trade finance tools due to limited legal and financial capacity in cross-border contexts (Zhou, Deng and Gibson, 2020).

Table 1.8 summarises the key differences in trade credit strategies between MNCs and SMEs, particularly in the context of the country effect. It highlights how organisational structure, resource availability and institutional variability impact each group's approach to managing trade credit risk in international contexts.

In sum, the country effect – through its institutional, economic, cultural and regulatory dimensions – significantly shapes firms' short-term financing behaviour. As global trade expands, understanding and adapting to national credit environments becomes increasingly important for financial decision-making and liquidity management.

1.6 Contemporary challenges to financial liquidity management

The short-term financing behaviour of firms is increasingly exposed to a range of macroeconomic, geopolitical and sustainability-related

Table 1.8 Country effect in trade credit strategies: MNCs vs. SMEs

Area	*MNCs*	*SMEs*
Credit policy approach	Adaptive; decentralised by local subsidiaries	Reactive; case-by-case basis
Decision-making structure	Delegated to regional offices to better adapt to local market specificity	Centralised but constrained by resource limitations
Institutional risk management	Reliance on in-house legal, compliance and risk management departments to interpret and manage country-specific regulations, enforce credit terms and mitigate exposure to legal, tax, or enforcement risks across jurisdictions	Dependence on external legal and financial advice, as well as trade finance instruments such as export insurance, factoring, or letters of credit, to manage regulatory uncertainty and mitigate credit risk in unfamiliar markets
Cultural adaptation	Guided by corporate policies but flexible	High sensitivity; reliance on local norms and trust-based deals
Trade finance tools used	Letters of credit, export guarantees, internal hedging	Export insurance, factoring, partner credit facilitation
Cross-border challenges	Complex but manageable through resources	Significant challenge arising from limited legal knowledge, high transaction costs and administrative burdens
Data and credit assessment	Integrated global systems (Enterprise Resource Planning, credit bureaus)	Limited access to structured credit information
Strategic focus	Optimising working capital efficiency globally	Minimising default risk and transaction costs
Response to country effect	Policy adjustment based on country-specific risk assessments	High reliance on partner trust and bilateral agreements

Source: Own compilation based on: Usai and Vannini (2005); Yeyati *et al.* (2007); Doole and Lowe (2008); Grant and Venzin (2009); Belghitar and Mateus (2016); Canto-Cuevas, Palacín-Sánchez and Di Pietro (2019); Zhou, Deng and Gibson (2020).

developments that redefine corporate liquidity management. While past research has extensively analysed the impacts of cyclical downturns and financial crises, recent disruptions – including the COVID-19 pandemic – have prompted a reassessment of both structural vulnerabilities and the resilience of corporate financing strategies (Demir and Javorcik, 2020; Fan *et al.*, 2021).

Corporate short-term finance has long been sensitive to macroeconomic disruptions. Yet, the recent succession of global crises – particularly the 2008 GFC and the COVID-19 pandemic – has exerted an unprecedented influence on the strategic and operational frameworks of short-term financial decision-making. These exogenous shocks have revealed and intensified vulnerabilities in firms' liquidity profiles, access to working capital and reliance on short-term borrowing, compelling enterprises to recalibrate their financing mechanisms in both reactive and preventative manners. The empirical evidence from multiple jurisdictions and sectors demonstrates that during such turbulent periods, short-term financial practices do not merely undergo temporary adjustment, but often experience structural transformation in response to external pressures, shifts in investor expectations and changes in financial intermediation practices. This crisis-induced reconfiguration of short-term finance is reflected in the academic literature. Pattnaik *et al.* (2020) report that nearly 70% of trade credit research emerged after the 2008 GFC, reflecting both its practical importance and repositioning as a core topic in finance, operations and supply chain disciplines.

During the 2008 GFC, the collapse of interbank lending and a dramatic spike in risk aversion led to a severe contraction in short-term credit availability, especially for firms lacking strong credit histories or collateral. The crisis exposed the fragility of overly leveraged financial structures and induced regulatory interventions that aimed to curtail excessive reliance on short-term debt markets (Ivashina and Scharfstein, 2010). As such, firms operating with short-term financing as a strategic lever – especially those with highly dynamic working capital requirements – found themselves in an unstable position. In many cases, they were forced to seek alternative liquidity channels or to liquidate assets at unfavourable terms, with potentially lasting repercussions for their operational continuity and creditworthiness.

Ivashina and Scharfstein (2010) document the severe dislocations in bank lending during the 2008 GFC, identifying a critical vulnerability rooted in banks' dependence on short-term funding. Their study reveals that banks relying more heavily on short-term creditors and less on deposit funding experienced sharper contractions in syndicated loan issuance following the collapse of Lehman Brothers. This dual liquidity shock – comprising both creditor withdrawals and borrower drawdowns – effectively constituted a modern-day bank run, one that drained systemic liquidity and intensified credit tightening. These findings confirmed growing concerns about maturity mismatches and rollover risk in bank balance sheets, ultimately informing the Basel Committee's decision to introduce stricter liquidity regulations in the form of the Liquidity Coverage Ratio (LCR) and Net Stable Funding Ratio (NSFR) under Basel III (Basel Committee on Banking Supervision, 2013, 2014). As framed by the Basel III reforms, the LCR requires banks to hold sufficient high-quality liquid assets to withstand a 30-day stress scenario, directly targeting the type of funding collapse identified by Ivashina and Scharfstein (2010). Meanwhile, the NSFR incentivises more stable, long-term funding structures, aiming to reduce the financial system's vulnerability to short-term debt market disruptions (Basel Committee on Banking Supervision, 2013).

The COVID-19 pandemic, however, presented a more complex and layered disruption. Unlike traditional financial crises caused by asset bubbles or sovereign defaults, the pandemic's shock was exogenous to the financial system, yet it had far-reaching effects across all channels of international commerce and financial liquidity. Corporate responses to this event in the field of short-term financing were marked by precautionary cash accumulation, unprecedented recourse to government-backed lending schemes and increased emphasis on cash flow forecasting.

The COVID-19 shock served as a catalyst for widespread liquidity shortages, disrupted supply chains and deteriorating sales, especially among SMEs. It led firms to increase their reliance on internal liquidity buffers and short-term credit, while facing tightened credit supply from formal financial institutions (Juergensen, Guimón and Narula, 2020). In this context, trade credit emerged once again as a critical counter-cyclical substitute for bank loans (Afrifa *et al.*, 2023), though its availability also varied considerably across sectors and countries.

Empirical evidence from a global sample of firms – including those in Europe and Asia – demonstrates a marked increase in precautionary borrowing behaviour and a strategic emphasis on renegotiating short-term credit lines during the COVID-19 pandemic, highlighting the key role of liquidity as the fundamental element of crisis-time financial resilience. Firms with greater cash reserves and access to undrawn credit facilities exhibited considerably stronger stock market performance, revealing the market's sensitivity to liquidity metrics during operational uncertainty and revenue declines (Ding *et al.*, 2021).

In examining corporate finance behaviour during crises, one of the clearest observations is that firms generally prioritise liquidity over cost-efficiency, thereby temporarily discarding traditional principles of capital optimisation. Demirgüç-Kunt, Martinez Peria and Tressel (2020) provide empirical evidence that, during the GFC, firms – particularly SMEs – shifted away from long-term debt issuance and increasingly relied on short-term borrowing mechanisms. This adjustment was not typically driven by strategic realignment, but rather by restricted access to long-term capital in the period of heightened financial uncertainty, increasing risk premiums and reluctance from both lenders and borrowers to engage in long-term commitments. Their findings reveal that such crisis-induced reallocation of financing preferences was especially pronounced in institutional contexts with weaker banking systems, lower credit information coverage and less efficient insolvency frameworks.

Complementing this global perspective, Hundal, Sandstrom and Uskumbayeva (2018) offer region-specific insights from Nordic countries, revealing that even relatively stable economies experienced a post-crisis shift towards higher leverage. According to their study, Nordic firms expanded debt positions, particularly short-term liabilities, due to falling interest rates, deteriorating equity market conditions and the necessity to stabilise liquidity positions in the face of continued macroeconomic uncertainty. These tendencies underline the crisis-induced compulsion to adjust financing structures reactively, rather than proactively. This shift led to an observable increase in short-term debt ratios, particularly among SMEs that lacked access to bond markets or international capital sources. The disproportionate effect on SMEs has been well-documented; these firms experienced both heightened financing costs and reduced willingness to lend from financial institutions (Ramdhan *et al.*, 2024).

This asymmetric impact is also supported by Abdulla, Dang and Khurshed (2017), who show that private firms rely more heavily on trade credit than public firms due to limited access to capital markets. However, during the GFC, these firms experienced a sharper decline in trade credit availability, revealing the fragility of supplier financing during systemic shocks and its uneven distribution across ownership structures.

The literature also indicates that the adverse impact of crises on short-term finance is often mediated by firm-specific characteristics such as industry affiliation, capital intensity, ownership structure and existing leverage. For instance, capital-intensive firms in the logistics and manufacturing sectors reported significant increases in receivables and inventories during the pandemic, thereby exerting additional strain on short-term liquidity (Papiernik-Wojdera and Pisarek-Bartoszewska, 2024). Moreover, the need to maintain supply chain fluidity in spite of falling revenues led to extended trade credit terms, further aggravating working capital imbalances.

Zhang (2020) confirms this perspective by showing that during the GFC, suppliers placed greater emphasis on conservative financial reporting when determining trade credit terms. The study reveals that conditional conservatism in borrowers' accounting enhanced their access to supplier credit, although this effect diminished in closely integrated supplier–buyer relationships or standardised transaction settings, suggesting crisis-induced shifts in supplier risk appetite.

In contrast, firms with stronger governance structures, diversified supply chains and prudent liquidity buffers were better equipped to withstand the short-term financial strains induced by crisis events. These firms not only maintained access to revolving credit facilities but were also more agile in redirecting internal capital and managing payables strategically. Dewally, Liu and Shao (2025) further argue that social responsibility and Environmental, Social, and Governance (ESG) orientation became amplifiers of financial resilience during the COVID-19 crisis, with such firms exhibiting stronger trade credit dynamics and more favourable borrowing conditions.

These firm-level patterns were also shaped by national policy responses. Al-Hadi and Al-Abri (2022) show that COVID-19-induced monetary and fiscal interventions influenced trade credit behaviour across 56 countries, with monetary easing reducing reliance on trade credit while targeted fiscal stimulus – particularly for SMEs – facilitated its expansion.

A significant development during crisis periods is the intensification of short-termism, that is a behavioural phenomenon where firms disproportionately prioritise immediate solvency over long-term value creation. While this approach is not necessarily negative in survival scenarios, it tends to curtail R&D expenditure, delay strategic investments and increase exposure to rollover risks. Lavín Fernández and Mazza (2024) note that the obsession with short-term survival during the pandemic undermined firms' capacity to invest in innovation, thus potentially impairing long-term competitiveness. This strategic contraction is compounded by higher uncertainty in the macroeconomic and regulatory environments, which discourages the issuance of long-term debt and equity instruments.

The state intervention during crises is another factor that influences short-term financing practices. Governmental measures such as temporary suspension of debt repayments, subsidised interest rates and emergency liquidity facilities helped to alleviate the financial pressures on many enterprises during the COVID-19 period. Yet, such interventions also created a distortionary effect, encouraging firms to maintain or even expand short-term liabilities under the assumption of continued policy support. Pinto and Costa (2023) identify the European Central Bank's Pandemic Emergency Purchase Programme (PEPP) as a key enabler of short-term financial stability, particularly through its impact on bond spreads. However, they caution that the gradual withdrawal of such interventions could expose structural weaknesses in corporate balance sheets, potentially revealing structural vulnerabilities that were temporarily concealed by fiscal and monetary support.

It is also purposeful to consider the psychological and behavioural dimensions of corporate financial management under crisis conditions. Panetsidou and Synapis (2024) demonstrate that financial managers exhibited heightened risk aversion and a reluctance to engage in external equity financing, despite accommodative market conditions during the latter stages of the COVID-19 pandemic. This behavioural rigidity often resulted in suboptimal capital allocation and increased reliance on bank overdrafts and short-term revolving credit – mechanisms typically associated with higher volatility and cost compared to medium- or long-term debt structures. This vulnerability is empirically supported by Duchin, Ozbas and Sensoy (2010), who find that investment activity during the subprime crisis contracted most severely among firms with low cash reserves and high short-term debt obligations, demonstrating the fragility of external finance dependence during systemic shocks.

Regional variations in the consequences of crises on short-term corporate finance further enrich the academic discourse. In emerging markets, for example, firms faced the dual constraints of underdeveloped financial systems and limited government support, thereby increasing their reliance on informal or internal financing mechanisms (Utz *et al.*, 2020). Supporting this view, Ding *et al.* (2023) find that firms with social connections to their suppliers – specifically through shared managers or directors – gain improved access to trade credit, particularly under heightened financial constraints. Their analysis of

Chinese-listed firms during the GFC highlights the growing importance of relationship-based informal financing when formal credit conditions deteriorate.

Carletti *et al.* (2020) document how European firms, particularly in Italy, responded to the liquidity strain induced by the pandemic by increasing reliance on short-term borrowing and actively drawing down revolving credit facilities. These asset-liability adjustments were primarily defensive, aimed at preserving cash flow continuity, especially in sectors exposed to revenue volatility. In contrast, broader access to institutional support mechanisms across the eurozone, including emergency liquidity schemes and credit guarantees, provided a stabilising buffer, allowing many firms to maintain short-term solvency without resorting to extreme deleveraging or asset fire sales. European firms were supported by centralised liquidity interventions such as the European Central Bank's PEPP and the third series of targeted longer-term refinancing operations (TLTRO-III), which ensured continued access to credit and emergency funding during peak disruption (European Central Bank, 2020).

Another remarkable trend observed in the wake of recent crises is the increasing integration of fintech solutions in short-term finance strategies. Digital lending platforms and supply chain financing technologies gained prominence as conventional credit channels became constrained. Ramdhan *et al.* (2024) document the rise of alternative lending models that enabled quicker access to credit, although often at higher risk-adjusted cost. The growing digitisation of cash flow management and forecasting tools also allowed firms to improve real-time visibility into their liquidity positions, which proved invaluable in responding to a crisis.

Supporting this view, Liu and Wang (2023) find that digital transformation not only enhances firms' operational transparency but also improves access to short-term bank credit, thereby increasing the firm's capacity to extend trade credit. Their findings suggest that digitally advanced firms are more resilient in times of crisis, as they are better positioned to reallocate liquidity through trade credit mechanisms.

Moreover, firms have become increasingly reliant on stress testing and scenario analysis to prepare for future disruptions, incorporating these tools into their treasury operations and financial planning cycles. The widespread adoption of such analytical mechanisms post-crisis suggests a maturing of the corporate finance function, where contingency planning is no longer an auxiliary activity but a core strategic necessity. Adebayo *et al.* (2025) highlight how the adoption of advanced predictive analytics and digital treasury tools enabled multinational firms to anticipate liquidity shortfalls and enhance short-term financial planning, especially under the pressure of disrupted capital flows during the pandemic.

It is also important to acknowledge that while crises often provoke reactive shifts in short-term financial strategies, they also stimulate enduring reform. The aftermath of COVID-19, for instance, witnessed a re-evaluation of key performance indicators in financial reporting, with increased emphasis on liquidity ratios, cash burn rates and short-term coverage metrics (Dorsman and Westerman, 2021). In response to the heightened uncertainty and economic disruption caused by the COVID-19 pandemic, European banks adjusted their internal credit rating assignments, often downgrading corporate exposures and incorporating more forward-looking indicators of financial distress into their assessments (Barmeier and Haller, 2022).

Beyond the pandemic, inflationary shocks have altered the cost of capital and constrained credit supply. Energy market volatility, fiscal stimulus and supply bottlenecks have driven global inflation, prompting monetary tightening and raising short-term borrowing costs – particularly for credit-constrained firms (Goodhart and Pradhan, 2020).

Geopolitical tensions, especially the Russia–Ukraine war, have introduced persistent uncertainty into financial markets and cross-border capital flows, further complicating liquidity planning in sectors exposed to commodity cycles or export dependencies (Crozet and Hinz, 2020). Simultaneously, trade disruptions linked to shifts in US tariff policy and the reconfiguration of supply chains have increased financing needs for inventory and receivables, while intensifying political risk in trade finance markets (Amiti and Weinstein, 2011; Fan *et al.*, 2021).

Another transformative trend is the growing integration of sustainability into financial decision-making. ESG criteria and the Sustainable Development Goals are increasingly incorporated into credit assessments, influencing firms' short-term borrowing costs and financial disclosure obligations (Krueger, Sautner and Starks, 2020; Berg, Kölbel and Rigobon, 2022). Institutions now condition access to short-term credit on ESG metrics, thereby reshaping incentives for working capital management and liquidity risk strategies (Delis *et al.*, 2024). This institutional turn is further supported by regulatory instruments such as the EU Taxonomy and the Corporate Sustainability Reporting Directive, which increase the transparency burden and expand the scope of financial accountability. As a result, short-term financing behaviour is increasingly co-determined by financial fundamentals and sustainability-driven governance mechanisms (Schoenmaker and Schramade, 2019).

In sum, crises, pandemics and other external pressures act as both stressors and drivers in the area of corporate short-term finance. They expose concealed weaknesses, accelerate digital and strategic innovation and reshape the behavioural contours of financial decision-making. While some firms emerge from such periods with enhanced resilience and renewed financial agility, others become trapped in cycles of short-termism and structural imbalance. The empirical and theoretical evidence reveals the necessity for firms to develop adaptable, data-informed and multidimensional short-term financing policies that are not merely reactive, but strategically anticipatory of external shocks.

References

Abdulla, Y., Dang, V.A. and Khurshed, A. (2017) 'Stock market listing and the use of trade credit: Evidence from public and private firms', *Journal of Corporate Finance*, 46, pp. 391–410. Available at: https://doi.org/10.1016/j.jcorpfin.2017.08.004.

Abuhommous, A.A.A. (2017) 'The impact of offering trade credit on firms' profitability', *Journal of Corporate Accounting and Finance*, 28(6), pp. 29–40. Available at: https://doi.org/10.1002/jcaf.22298.

Accominotti, O. and Ugolini, S. (2019) 'International trade finance from the origins to the present: Market structures, regulation, and governance ', in E. Brousseau, J.-M. Glachant, and J. Sgard (eds) *The Oxford Handbook of Institutions of International Economic Governance and Market Regulation*. online edn. Oxford Academic.

Acharya, V. V., Almeida, H. and Campello, M. (2013) 'Aggregate risk and the choice between cash and lines of credit', *Journal of Finance*, 68(5), pp. 2059–2116.

Adebayo, O. *et al.* (2025) 'Impact of digital transformation on liquidity management among U.S. multinational corporations', *International Journal for Multidisciplinary Research*, 7(2), pp. 1–13. Available at: www.ijfmr.com.

Afrifa, G.A. *et al.* (2023) 'Do trade credit and bank credit complement or substitute each other in public and private firms?', *International Review of Economics and Finance*, 88, pp. 748–765. Available at: https://doi.org/10.1016/j.iref.2023.07.017.

Agostino, M. and Trivieri, F. (2014) 'Does trade credit play a signalling role? Some evidence from SMEs microdata', *Small Business Economics*, 42(1), pp. 131–151. Available at: https://doi.org/10.1007/s11187-013-9478-8.

Aguiar-Díaz, I., Mruk, E. and Ruiz-Mallorquí, M.V. (2024) 'How judicial efficiency impacts trade credit and doubtful receivables', *European Journal of Law and Economics*, 57, pp. 63–91. Available at: https://doi.org/10.1007/s10657-024-09793-0.

Ahmed, J., Xiaofeng, H. and Khalid, J. (2014) 'Determinants of trade credit: The case of a developing economy', *European Researcher*, 83(9–2), pp. 1694–1706. Available at: https://doi.org/10.13187/er.2014.83.1694.

Akang, A.U. (2023) 'Regulatory compliance and access to finance: Implications for business growth in developing economies', *Sciental Journal of Education Humanities and Social Sciences*, 1(2), pp. 8–23. Available at: https://doi.org/10.62536/sjehss.2023.v1.i2.pp8-23.

Alarcón, L.S. (2011) 'The trade credit in the Spanish agrofood industry', *Mediterranean Journal of Economics, Agriculture and Environment,* 10(2), pp. 51–57.

Al-Hadi, A. and Al-Abri, A. (2022) 'Firm-level trade credit responses to COVID-19-induced monetary and fiscal policies: International evidence', *Research in International Business and Finance*, 60. Available at: https://doi.org/10.1016/j.ribaf.2021.101568.

Amiti, M. and Weinstein, D.E. (2011) 'Exports and financial shocks', *The Quarterly Journal of Economics*, 126(4), pp. 1841–1877. Available at: http://hdl.handle.net/10.1093/qje/qjr03

Andrieu, G., Staglianò, R. and van der Zwan, P. (2018) 'Bank debt and trade credit for SMEs in Europe: firm-, industry-, and country-level determinants', *Small Business Economics*, 51(1), pp. 245–264. Available at: https://doi.org/10.1007/s11187-017-9926-y.

Angori, G. and Aristei, D. (2022) 'Heterogeneity and state dependence in firms access to credit', *Small Business Economics*, 59, pp. 47–78. https://doi.org/10.1007/s11187-021-00545-x

Atanasova, C. (2007) 'Access to institutional finance and the use of trade credit', *Financial Management*, 36(1), pp. 49–67.

Avalos, F., Doerr, S. and Pinter, G. (2025) 'The global drivers of private credit', *BIS Quarterly Review*, pp. 13–30.

Bărbuţă-Mişu, N. (2018) 'Analysis of factors influencing managerial decision to use trade credit in construction sector', *Economic Research-Ekonomska Istraživanja*, 31(1), pp. 1903–1922.

Barmeier, M. and Haller, M. (2022) 'Changes in banks' rating assignments in response to the COVID-19 pandemic', *Financial Stability Report.* Oesterreichische Nationalbank.

Barrot, J.N. (2016) 'Trade credit and industry dynamics: Evidence from trucking firms', *Journal of Finance*, 71(5), pp. 1975–2016. Available at: https://doi.org/10.1111/jofi.12371.

Basel Committee on Banking Supervision (2013) *Basel III: The liquidity coverage ratio and liquidity risk monitoring tools.*

Basel Committee on Banking Supervision (2014) *Basel III: The net stable funding Ratio.*

Bastos, R. and Pindado, J. (2013) 'Trade credit during a financial crisis: A panel data analysis', *Journal of Business Research*, 66(5), pp. 614–620. Available at: https://doi.org/10.1016/j.jbusres.2012.03.015.

Beck, T., Demirgüç-Kunt, A. and Maksimovic, V. (2008) 'Financing patterns around the world: Are small firms different?', *Journal of Financial Economics*, 89, pp. 467–487. Available at: https://www.sciencedirect.com/science/article/abs/pii/S0304405X08000986.

Belghitar, Y. and Mateus, C. (2016) 'Trade credit in Europe: "It is all down to culture"', *SSRN Electronic Journal* [Preprint], (December 2017). Available at: https://doi.org/10.2139/ssrn.2809112.

Berg, F., Kölbel, J.F. and Rigobon, R. (2022) 'Aggregate confusion: The divergence of ESG ratings', *Review of Finance*, 26(6), pp. 1315–1344. Available at: https://doi.org/10.1093/rof/rfac033.

Berger, A.N. and Udell, G.F. (2006) 'A more complete conceptual framework for SME finance', *Journal of Banking & Finance*, 30(11), pp. 2945–2966.

Bertrand, J. and Murro, P. (2022) 'Firm–bank "odd couples" and trade credit: Evidence from Italian small- and medium-sized enterprises', *Economic Modelling*, 111, p. 105829. Available at: https://doi.org/10.1016/J.ECONMOD.2022.105829.

Biais, B. and Gollier, C. (1997) 'Trade credit and credit rationing', *Review of Financial Studies*, 10(4), pp. 903–937. Available at: https://www.jstor.org/stable/2962334.

Białek-Jaworska, A. and Nehrebecka, N. (2016) 'The role of trade credit in business operations', *Argumenta Oeconomica*, 37(2), pp. 189–231. Available at: https://doi.org/10.15611/aoe.2016.2.08.

Bilyay-Erdogan, S. and Öztürkkal, B. (2023) 'The role of environmental, social, governance (ESG) practices and ownership on firm performance in emerging markets', *Emerging Markets Finance and Trade*, 59(12), pp. 3776–3797. Available at: https://doi.org/https://doi.org/10.1080/1540496X.2023.2223930.

Boot, A.W.A. (2000) 'Relationship banking: What do we know?', *Journal of Financial Intermediation*, 9(1), pp. 7–25. Available at: https://doi.org/10.1006/jfin.2000.0282.

Bougheas, S., Mateut, S. and Mizen, P. (2009) 'Corporate trade credit and inventories: New evidence of a trade-off from accounts payable and receivable', *Journal of Banking and Finance*, 33(2), pp. 300–307. Available at: https://doi.org/10.1016/j.jbankfin.2008.07.019.

Brealey, R.A., Myers, S.C. and Allen, F. (2020) *Principles of Corporate Finance. 13th Edition.* 13th ed. New York, NY: McGraw-Hill Education.

Brennan, M.J., Maksimovics, V. and Zechner, J. (1988) 'Vendor financing', *Journal of Finance*, 43(5), pp. 1127–1141. Available at: https://doi.org/10.2307/2328210.

Burkart, M. and Ellingsen, T. (2004) 'In-kind finance: A theory of trade credit', *American Economic Review*, 94(3), pp. 569–590. Available at: https://doi.org/10.1257/0002828041464579.

Bussoli, C. and Marino, F. (2018) 'Trade credit in times of crisis: Evidence from European SMEs', *Journal of Small Business and Enterprise Development*, 25(10), pp. 277–293.

Caglio, C.R., Darst, R.M. and Kalemli-Özcan, Şebnem (2021) *Collateral Heterogeneity and Monetary Policy Transmission: Evidence from Loans to SMEs and Large Firms*. 28685. Available at: http://www.nber.org/papers/w28685.

Cai, G., Chen, X. and Xiao, Z. (2014) 'The roles of bank and trade credits: Theoretical analysis and empirical evidence', *Production and Operations Management*, 23(4), pp. 583–598. Available at: https://doi.org/https://doi.org/10.1111/poms.12035.

Cantero Sáiz, M. *et al.* (2017) 'Trade credit, sovereign risk and monetary policy in Europe', *International Review of Economics and Finance*, 52, pp. 39–54. Available at: https://doi.org/10.1016/j.iref.2017.09.010.

Canto-Cuevas, F.J., Palacín-Sánchez, M.J. and di Pietro, F. (2016) 'Trade credit in SMEs: A quantile regression approach', *Applied Economics Letters*, 23(13), pp. 945–948. Available at: https://doi.org/10.1080/13504851.2015.1122727.

Canto-Cuevas, F.J., Palacín-Sánchez, M.J. and Di Pietro, F.D. (2019) 'Trade credit as a sustainable resource during an SME's life cycle', *Sustainability*, 11(3), pp. 1–16. Available at: www.mdpi.com/2071-1050/11/3/670.

Carbó-Valverde, S., Rodríguez-Fernández, F. and Udell, G.F. (2016) 'Trade credit, the financial crisis, and SME access to finance', *Journal of Money, Credit and Banking*, 48(1), pp. 113–143.

Carbo-Valverde, S., Udell, G.F. and Rodríguez-Fernández, F. (2011) 'Bank market power and SME financing constraints', *SSRN Electronic Journal* [Preprint]. Available at: https://doi.org/10.2139/ssrn.910226.

Carletti, E. *et al.* (2020) 'The COVID-19 shock and equity shortfall: Firm-level evidence from Italy', *Review of Corporate Finance Studies*, 9(3), pp. 534–568. Available at: https://doi.org/10.1093/rcfs/cfaa014.

Carvalho, C.J. de and Schiozer, R. (2015) 'Determinants of supply and demand for trade credit by micro, small and medium-sized enterprises', *Revista Contabilidade & Finanças*, 26(68), pp. 208–222. Available at: https://doi.org/10.1590/1808-057x201500940.

Casey, E. and O'Toole, C.M. (2014) 'Bank lending constraints, trade credit and alternative financing during the financial crisis: Evidence from European SMEs', *Journal of Corporate Finance*, 27, pp. 173–193. Available at: https://doi.org/10.1016/J.JCORPFIN.2014.05.001.

Castaldo, A. *et al.* (2023) 'Access to bank financing and start-up resilience: A survival analysis across business sectors in a time of crisis', *Manchester School*, 91(3), pp. 141–170. Available at: https://doi.org/10.1111/manc.12433.

Chapman, S.D. (1984) *The Rise of Merchant Banking*. London: Allen & Unwin.

Chod, J., Lyandres, E. and Yang, S.A. (2019) 'Trade credit and supplier competition', *Journal of Financial Economics*, 131(2), pp. 484–505. Available at: https://doi.org/10.1016/j.jfineco.2018.08.008.

Chodorow-Reich, G. *et al.* (2022) 'Bank liquidity provision across the firm size distribution', *Journal of Financial Economics*, 144(3), pp. 908–932. Available at: https://doi.org/10.1016/J.JFINECO.2021.06.035.

Claessens, S. and Klapper, L.F. (2005) 'Bankruptcy around the world: Explanations of its relative use', *American Law and Economics Review*, 7(1), pp. 253–283.

Cole, R.A. (2010) 'Bank credit, trade credit or no credit: Evidence from the surveys of small business finances', *US Small Business Administration Research Study*, 365, pp. 1–49. Available at: https://papers.ssrn.com/sol3/papers.cfm?abstract_id=1540221.

Costa, M.D. and Habib, A. (2021) 'Trade credit and cost stickiness', *Accounting and Finance*, 61, pp. 1139–1179. Available at: https://doi.org/10.1111/acfi.12606.

Cowton, C.J. and San-Jose, L. (2017) 'On the ethics of trade credit: Understanding good payment practice in the supply chain', *Journal of Business Ethics*, 140(4), pp. 673–685. Available at: https://doi.org/10.1007/s10551-016-3050-9.

Crozet, M. and Hinz, J. (2020) 'Friendly fire: The trade impact of the Russia sanctions and counter-sanctions', *Economic Policy*, 35(101):97-146(101), pp. 97–146. Available at: https://doi.org/10.1093/epolic/eiaa006.

Cull, R., Xu, L.C. and Zhu, T. (2009) 'Formal finance and trade credit during China's transition', *Journal of Financial Intermediation*, 18(2), pp. 173–192. Available at: https://doi.org/10.1016/J.JFI.2008.08.004.

Cuñat, V. (2007) 'Trade credit: Suppliers as debt collectors and insurance providers', *Review of Financial Studies*, 20(2), pp. 491–527. Available at: https://www.jstor.org/stable/4494777.

Cunningham, R.M. (2005) 'Trade credit and credit rationing in Canadian firms', *Bank of Canada Working Paper No. 2004-49* [Preprint]. Available at: https://doi.org/http://dx.doi.org/10.2139/ssrn.643023.

Danielson, M.G. and Scott, J.A. (2004) 'Bank loan availability and trade credit demand', *Financial Review*, 39(4), pp. 579–600. Available at: https://doi.org/10.1111/j.0732-8516.2004.00089.x.

Delis, M.D. *et al.* (2024) 'Being stranded with fossil fuel reserves? Climate policy risk and the pricing of bank loans', *Financial Markets, Institutions and Instruments*, 33(3), pp. 239–265. Available at: https://doi.org/10.1111/fmii.12189.

Deloof, M. and Jegers, M. (1996) 'Trade credit, product quality, and intragroup trade: some European evidence', *Financial Management*, 25(3), pp. 33–43. Available at: www.jstor.org/stable/3665806.

Deloof, M. and Jegers, M. (1999) 'Trade credit, corporate groups, and the financing of Belgian firms', *Journal of Business Finance & Accounting*, 26(7–8), pp. 945–966. Available at: https://doi.org/https://doi.org/10.1111/1468-5957.00281.

Deloof, M. and La Rocca, M. (2015) 'Local financial development and the trade credit policy of Italian SMEs', *Small Business Economics*, 44(4), pp. 905–924. Available at: https://doi.org/10.1007/s11187-014-9617-x.

Demir, B. and Javorcik, B. (2020) 'Trade finance matters: Evidence from the COVID-19 crisis', *Oxford Review of Economic Policy*, 36, pp. S397–S408. Available at: https://doi.org/10.1093/oxrep/graa034.

Demirguc-Kunt, A. and Maksimovic, V. (2001) 'Firms as financial intermediaries – evidence from trade credit data', *Policy Research Working Paper Series 2696, The World Bank*, 2696.

Demirgüç-Kunt, A., Martinez Peria, M.S. and Tressel, T. (2020) 'The global financial crisis and the capital structure of firms: Was the impact more severe among SMEs and non-listed firms?', *Journal of Corporate Finance*, 60, p. 101514. Available at: https://doi.org/10.1016/J.JCORPFIN.2019.101514.

Dewally, M., Liu, P. and Shao, Y. (2025) 'Extending trade credit as socially responsible companies: evidence from the COVID-19 pandemic ', *International Journal of Managerial Finance*, ahead-of-print(ahead-of-print).

Diamond, D.W. (1991) 'Monitoring and reputation: The choice between bank loans and directly placed debt', *Journal of Political Economy*, 99(4), pp. 689–721.

Ding, F. *et al.* (2023) 'Firms' access to informal financing: The role of shared managers in trade credit access', *Journal of Corporate Finance*, 79. Available at: https://doi.org/10.1016/j.jcorpfin.2023.102388.

Ding, W. *et al.* (2021) 'Corporate immunity to the COVID-19 pandemic', *Journal of Financial Economics*, 141(2), pp. 802–830. Available at: https://doi.org/10.1016/j.jfineco.2021.03.005.

Doole, I. and Lowe, R. (2008) *International marketing strategy: analysis, development and implementation*. 5th edn. London: Cengage Learning.

Dorsman, A.B. and Westerman, W. (2021) 'Corporate liquidity in normal and crisis times: What is the best yardstick?', *The Central European Review of Economics and Management*, 5(4), pp. 9–32. Available at: https://doi.org/10.29015/cerem.927.

Duchin, R., Ozbas, O. and Sensoy, B.A. (2010) 'Costly external finance, corporate investment, and the subprime mortgage credit crisis', *Journal of*

Financial Economics, 97(3), pp. 418–435. Available at: https://doi.org/10.1016/J.JFINECO.2009.12.008.

Duliniec, A. and Świda, N. (2021) 'Factors influencing the use of trade credit in financing Polish listed companies', *Economics and Business Review*, 7(21), pp. 113–134. Available at: https://doi.org/10.18559/ebr.2021.1.7.

Engemann, M., Eck, K. and Schnitzer, M. (2014) 'Trade credits and bank credits in international trade: Substitutes or complements?', *World Economy*, 37(11), pp. 1507–1540. Available at: https://doi.org/10.1111/twec.12167.

European Central Bank (2020) 'Economic and monetary developments', *ECB Economic Bulletin* [Preprint]. European Central Bank.

Fabbri, D. and Klapper, L.F. (2016) 'Bargaining power and trade credit', *Journal of Corporate Finance*, 41, pp. 66–80. Available at: https://doi.org/10.1016/j.jcorpfin.2016.07.001.

Fan, D., Zhou, Y., Yeung, A.C.L., Lo, Ch.K.Y. and Tang, Ch. (2021) 'Impact of the U.S.-China trade war on the operating performance of U.S. firms: The role of outsourcing and supply base complexity', *Journal of Operations Management*, 68(8), pp. 928–962.

Fazzari, S.M., Hubbard, R.G. and Petersen, B.C. (1988) 'Financing constraints and corporate investment', *Brookings Papers on Economic Activity*, pp. 141–206. Available at: https://doi.org/https://doi.org/10.2307/2534426.

Fazzari, S.M. and Petersen, B.C. (1993) 'Working capital and fixed investment: New evidence on financing constraints', *The RAND Journal of Economics*, 24(3), pp. 328–342. Available at: www.jstor.org/stable/2555961.

Ferrando, A. and Mulier, K. (2013) 'Do firms use the trade credit channel to manage growth?', *Journal of Banking and Finance*, 37(8), pp. 3035–3046. Available at: https://doi.org/10.1016/j.jbankfin.2013.02.013.

Ferris, J.S. (1981) 'A transactions theory of trade credit use', *Quarterly Journal of Economics*, 96(2), pp. 243–270. Available at: https://doi.org/https://doi.org/10.2307/1882390.

Fisman, R. and Love, I. (2003) 'Trade credit, financial intermediary development, and industry growth', *Journal of Finance*, 58(1), pp. 353–374.

Fisman, R. and Raturi, M. (2004) 'Does competition encourage credit provision? Evidence from African trade credit relationships', *Review of Economics and Statistics*, 86(1), pp. 345–352. Available at: https://doi.org/10.1162/003465304323023859.

Frank, M.Z. and Goyal, V.K. (2009) 'Capital structure decisions: Which factors are reliably important?', *Financial Management*, 38(1), pp. 1–37.

Fukuda, S.I., Kasuya, M. and Akashi, K. (2006) *The role of trade credit for small firms: An implication from Japan's banking crisis*, *Japan Public Policy Review*. CIRJE-F-440.

Garcia-Appendini, E. and Montoriol-Garriga, J. (2013) 'Firms as liquidity providers: Evidence from the 2007-2008 financial crisis', *Journal of*

Financial Economics, 109(1), pp. 272–291. Available at: https://doi.org/10.1016/j.jfineco.2013.02.010.

García-Teruel, P.J. and Martínez-Solano, P. (2010) 'Determinants of trade credit: A comparative study of European SMEs', *International Small Business Journal*, 28(3), pp. 215–233. Available at: https://doi.org/10.1177/0266242609360603.

Ge, Y. and Qiu, J. (2007) 'Financial development, bank discrimination and trade credit', *Journal of Banking & Finance*, 31(2), pp. 513–530. Available at: https://doi.org/10.1016/J.JBANKFIN.2006.07.009.

Ghulam, Y., Hakro, A.N. and Naumani, O. (2025) 'SMEs' access to bank financing during the financial crises in Europe', *Journal of Small Business Strategy*, 35(1), pp. 74–96. Available at: https://doi.org/10.53703/001c.124820.

Giannetti, M., Burkart, M. and Ellingsen, T. (2011) 'What you sell is what you lend? Explaining trade credit contracts', *Review of Financial Studies*, 24(4), pp. 1261–1298. Available at: https://doi.org/10.1093/rfs/hhn096.

Gongeta, S. (2024) 'New European regime for combatting late payments in commercial transactions – Key elements of revision after a decade', *EU and comparative law issues and challenges series*, 8, pp. 390–414. Available at: https://doi.org/10.25234/eclic/32284.

Goodhart, C. and Pradhan, M. (2020) *The Great Demographic Reversal: Ageing Societies, Waning Inequality, and an Inflation Revival*. London: Springer.

Grant, R.M. and Venzin, M. (2009) 'Strategic and organisational challenges of internationalisation in financial services', *Long Range Planning*, 42(5–6), pp. 561–587. Available at: https://doi.org/10.1016/j.lrp.2009.10.005.

Gur, N. *et al.* (2023) 'Firm size and financing behavior during COVID-19 pandemic: Evidence from SMEs in Istanbul', *Borsa Istanbul Review*, 23(4), pp. 804–817. Available at: https://doi.org/10.1016/j.bir.2023.02.001.

Harris, C., Roark, S. and Li, Z. (2019) 'Cash flow volatility and trade credit in Asia', *International Journal of Managerial Finance*, 15(2), pp. 257–271.

Hasan, M.M. and Alam, N. (2022) 'Asset redeployability and trade credit', *International Review of Financial Analysis*, 80, 102024. Available at: https://doi.org/10.1016/J.IRFA.2022.102024.

Hasan, M.M. and Habib, A. (2019) 'Social capital and trade credit', *International Review of Financial Analysis*, 61, pp. 158–174. Available at: https://doi.org/10.1016/J.IRFA.2018.10.002.

Hoang, C.H. *et al.* (2023) 'Does national culture impact trade credit provision of SMEs?', *Economic Modelling*, 124, 106288. Available at: https://doi.org/10.1016/J.ECONMOD.2023.106288.

Hoang, H.C., Xiao, Q. and Akbar, S. (2019) 'Trade credit, firm profitability, and financial constraints: Evidence from listed SMEs in East Asia and the Pacific', *International Journal of Managerial Finance*, 15(5), pp. 744–770. Available at: https://doi.org/10.1108/IJMF-09-2018-0258.

Hofstede, G. (2001) *Culture's Consequences. Comparing Values, Behaviors, Institutions, and Organizations Across Nations*. 2nd edn. Thousand Oaks, CA: Sage Publications.

Hui, H., Xiaojun, S. and Shunming, Z. (2011) 'Counter-cyclical substitution between trade credit and bank credit', *Journal of Banking & Finance*, 35(8), pp. 1859–1878. Available at: https://doi.org/https://doi.org/10.1016/j.jbankfin.2010.12.009.

Hundal, S., Sandstrom, A. and Uskumbayeva, A. (2018) 'The impact of the financial crisis on corporate capital structure dynamics in the Nordic countries', *Eurasian Journal of Economics and Finance*, 6(3), pp. 34–51. Available at: https://doi.org/10.15604/ejef.2018.06.03.003.

Huyghebaert, N. (2006) 'On the determinants and dynamics of trade credit use: Empirical evidence from business start-ups', *Journal of Business Finance and Accounting*, 33(1–2), pp. 305–328. Available at: https://onlinelibrary.wiley.com/doi/10.1111/j.1468-5957.2006.001364.x.

Huyghebaert, N., Van De Gucht, L. and Van Hulle, C. (2007) 'The choice between bank debt and trace credit in business start-ups', *Small Business Economics*, 29(4), pp. 435–452. Available at: https://doi.org/10.1007/s11187-006-9005-2.

Ivashina, V. and Scharfstein, D. (2010) 'Bank lending during the financial crisis of 2008', *Journal of Financial Economics*, 97(3), pp. 319–338. Available at: https://doi.org/10.1016/j.jfineco.2009.12.001.

Jou, J., Li, L. and Wang, T. (2024) 'Trade credit supply and usage during normal and crisis times: A review of recent literature', in F. Allen and M. Qian (eds) *Research Handbook on Alternative Finance*. Cheltenham, UK: Edward Elgar Publishing (Research Handbook of Alternative Finance), pp. 70–83. Available at: https://ssrn.com/abstract=4559352.

Juergensen, J., Guimón, J. and Narula, R. (2020) 'European SMEs amidst the COVID-19 crisis: Assessing impact and policy responses', *Journal of Industrial and Business Economics*, 47(3), pp. 499–510. Available at: https://doi.org/10.1007/s40812-020-00169-4.

Kaya, O. (2024) 'The impact of late payments on SMEs' access to finance: Evidence from credit rationing and loan terms', *Economic Modelling*, 141. Available at: https://doi.org/10.1016/j.econmod.2024.106896.

Kling, G., Salima, P. and Eleimon, G. (2011) 'Cash holding, trade credit and access to short-term bank finance', *International Review of Financial Analysis*, 32, pp. 123–131. Available at: https://doi.org/https://doi.org/10.1016/j.irfa.2014.01.013.

Kohler, M., Britton, E. and Yates, A. (2000) 'Trade credit and the monetary transmission mechanism', *The Bank of England Working Paper No. 115* [Preprint]. Available at: https://doi.org/http://dx.doi.org/10.2139/ssrn.234693.

Krueger, P., Sautner, Z. and Starks, L.T. (2020) 'The importance of climate risks for institutional investors', *The Review of Financial Studies*, 33(3), pp. 1067–1111. Available at: https://doi.org/10.1093/rfs/hhz137.

Laghari, F. and Chengang, Y. (2019) 'Investment in working capital and financial constraints: Empirical evidence on corporate performance', *International Journal of Managerial Finance*, 15(2), pp. 164–190. Available at: https://doi.org/10.1108/IJMF-10-2017-0236.

Lavín Fernández, A. and Mazza, C. (2024) 'Short-termism: What you could do tomorrow will largely depend on your doing today. In: . . Palgrave Macmillan, Cham. ', in *Boards Under Crisis*. Cham: IE Business Publishing. Palgrave Macmillan, pp. 45–67.

Lawrenz, J. and Oberndorfer, J. (2018) 'Firm size effects in trade credit supply and demand', *Journal of Banking and Finance*, 93, pp. 1–20. Available at: https://doi.org/10.1016/j.jbankfin.2018.05.014.

Lefebvre, V. (2023) 'Trade credit, payment duration, and SMEs' growth in the European Union', *International Entrepreneurship and Management Journal*, 19(3), pp. 1313–1340. Available at: https://doi.org/10.1007/s11 365-023-00871-4.

Lehar, A., Song, V.Y. and Yuan, L. (2020) 'Industry structure and the strategic provision of trade credit by upstream firms', *The Review of Financial Studies*, 33(10), pp. 4916–4972. Available at: https://ssrn.com/abstract=2143687.

Levine, R., Lin, C. and Xie, W. (2018) 'Corporate resilience to banking crises: The roles of trust and trade credit', *Journal of Financial and Quantitative Analysis*, 53(4), pp. 1441–1477. Available at: https://doi.org/ 10.1017/S0022109018000224.

Lin, T.T. and Chou, J.H. (2015) 'Trade credit and bank loan: Evidence from Chinese firms', *International Review of Economics and Finance*, 36, pp. 17–29. Available at: https://doi.org/10.1016/j.iref.2014.11.004.

Liu, G.Q. and Wang, S.H. (2023) 'Digital transformation and trade credit provision: evidence from China', *Research in International Business and Finance*, 64(C), 101805. https://ideas.repec.org/a/eee/riibaf/v64y2023ics0 27553192200191x.html

Love, I., Preve, L.A. and Sarria-Allende, V. (2007) 'Trade credit and bank credit: Evidence from recent financial crises', *Journal of Financial Economics*, 83(2), pp. 453–469. Available at: https://doi.org/10.1016/j.jfin eco.2005.11.002.

Love, I. and Zaidi, R. (2010) 'Trade credit, bank credit and financial crisis', *International Review of Finance*, 10(1), pp. 125–147.

Luo, H. (2022) 'COVID-19 and trade credit speed of adjustment', *Finance Research Letters*, 47. Available at: https://doi.org/10.1016/ j.frl.2021.102541.

Ma, C. and Fang, J. (2023) 'Does cross-industry loan diversification reduce bank systemic risk? Evidence from listed banks in China', *China Journal of Accounting Studies*, 11(4), pp. 719–755. Available at: https://doi.org/ 10.1080/21697213.2023.2300294.

Ma, L. and Ma, S. (2020) 'Trade credit use and bank loan access: An agency theory perspective', *Accounting and Finance*, 60(2), pp. 1835–1865. Available at: https://doi.org/10.1111/acfi.12517.

Machokoto, M., Gyimah, D. and Ibrahim, B.M. (2022) 'The evolution of trade credit: new evidence from developed versus developing countries', *Review of Quantitative Finance and Accounting*, 59(3), pp. 857–912. Available at: https://doi.org/10.1007/s11156-022-01061-z.

Maksimovic, V. and Frank, M.Z. (2005) 'Trade credit, collateral, and adverse selection', *SSRN Electronic Journal*, 96(1). Available at: https://doi.org/10.2139/ssrn.87868.

Marotta, G. (2005) 'When do trade credit discounts matter? Evidence from Italian firm-level data', *Applied Economics*, 37(4), pp. 403–416. Available at: https://doi.org/10.1080/0003684042000329063.

Martinez-Sola, C., García-Teruel, P.J. and Martinez-Solano, P. (2012) 'Corporate cash holding and firm value', *Applied Economics*, 45(2), pp. 161–170.

Martínez-Sola, C., García-Teruel, P.J. and Martínez-Solano, P. (2014) 'Trade credit and SME profitability', *Small Business Economics*, 42(3), pp. 561–577. Available at: https://doi.org/10.1007/s11187-013-9491-y.

Mateut, S. (2014) 'Reverse trade credit or default risk? Explaining the use of prepayments by firms', *Journal of Corporate Finance*, 29, pp. 303–326. Available at: https://doi.org/10.1016/j.jcorpfin.2014.09.009.

Mateut, S., Bougheas, S. and Mizen, P. (2006) 'Trade credit, bank lending and monetary policy transmission', *European Economic Review*, 50(3), pp. 603–629. Available at: https://doi.org/10.1016/J.EUROECOREV.2005.01.002.

Mateut, S. and Mizen, P. (2003) *Trade Credit and Bank Lending: An Investigation into the Determinants of UK Manufacturing Firms' Access to Trade Credit*. 2003/3. Available at: https://www.researchgate.net/publication/5020886.

McGuinness, G. and Hogan, T. (2014) 'Bank credit and trade credit: Evidence from SMEs over the financial crisis', *International Small Business Journal: Researching Entrepreneurship*, 34(4), pp. 412–445. Available at: https://doi.org/10.1177/0266242614558314.

McGuinness, G., Hogan, T. and Powell, R. (2018) 'European trade credit use and SME survival', *Journal of Corporate Finance*, 49, pp. 81–103. Available at: https://doi.org/10.1016/j.jcorpfin.2017.12.005.

McMillan, J. and Woodruff, C. (1999) 'Interfirm relationships and informal credit in Vietnam', *The Quarterly Journal of Economics*, 114(4), pp. 1285–1320. Available at: https://www.jstor.org/stable/2586964.

Meltzer, A.H. (1960) 'Mercantile credit, monetary policy, and size of firms', *Review of Economics and Statistics*, 42(4), pp. 429–437. Available at: https://doi.org/10.2307/1925692.

Mian, S.L. and Smith, C.W. (1992) 'Accounts receivable management policy: Theory and evidence', *Journal of Finance*, 47(1), pp. 169–200. Available at: https://doi.org/10.2307/2329094.

Molina, C.A. and Preve, L.A. (2009) 'Trade receivables policy of distressed firms and its effect on the costs of financial distress, financial management', 38(3), pp. 663-686. Available at: https://doi.org/10.1111/j.1755-053X.2009.01051.x

Molina, C.A. and Preve, L.A. (2012) 'An empirical analysis of the effect of financial distress on trade credit', *Financial Management*, 41(1), pp. 187–205. Available at: https://doi.org/10.1111/J.1755-053X.2012.01182.X.

Moro, A., Maresch, D. and Ferrando, A. (2018) 'Creditor protection, judicial enforcement and credit access', *European Journal of Finance*, 24(3), pp. 250–281. Available at: https://doi.org/10.1080/1351847X.2016.1216871.

Myers, S.C. and Majluf, N. (1984) 'Corporate financing and investment decisions when firms have information that investors do not have', *Journal of Financial Economics*, 13(2), pp. 187–221.

Ng, C.K., Smith, J.K. and Smith, R.L. (1999) 'Evidence on the determinants of credit terms used in interfirm trade', *Journal of Finance*, 54(3), pp. 1109–1129. Available at: https://doi.org/10.1111/0022-1082.00138.

Nilsen, J.H. (2002) 'Trade credit and the bank lending channel', *Journal of Money, Credit, and Banking*, 34(1), pp. 226–253. Available at: https://doi.org/10.1353/MCB.2002.0032.

Norden, L., Van Kampen, S. and Illueca, M. (2021) 'Credit quality and substitution in SME finance', *Journal of Financial Management, Markets and Institutions*, 9(1), pp. 1–26. Available at: https://doi.org/10.1142/S2282717X21500055.

OECD (2024) *Financing SMEs and Entrepreneurs 2024. An OECD Scoreboard*. Paris: OECD Publishing. Available at: https://doi.org/10.1787/fa521246-en. (Accessed: 19 March 2025).

Ogawa, K., Sterken, E. and Tokutsu, I. (2013) 'The trade credit channel revisited: Evidence from micro data of Japanese small firms', *Small Business Economics*, 40(1), pp. 101–118. Available at: https://doi.org/10.1007/S11187-011-9344-5.

Ono, M. (2001) 'Determinants of trade credit in the Japanese manufacturing sector', *Journal of the Japanese and International Economies*, 15(2), pp. 160–177. Available at: https://doi.org/https://doi.org/10.1006/jjie.2001.0466.

Opler, T. *et al.* (1999) 'The determinants and implications of corporate cash holdings', *Journal of Financial Economics*, 52(1), pp. 3–46. Available at: https://doi.org/10.1016/s0304-405x(99)00003-3.

Palacín-Sánchez, M., Canto-Cuevas, F. and Di-Pietro, F. (2019) 'Trade credit versus bank credit: A simultaneous analysis in European SMEs', *Small Business Economics*, 53(4), pp. 1079–1096. Available at: https://doi.org/10.1007/s11187-018-0101-x.

Panetsidou, S. and Synapis, A. (2024) 'Equity financing during the Covid-19 economic downturn accounting', *Review of Quantitative Finance and Accounting*, 64(3), pp. 1391–1430. Available at: https://www.washingtonpost.com/business/2020/05/08/april-2020-jobs-report/.

Papiernik-Wojdera, M. and Pisarek-Bartoszewska, R. (2024) 'Credit position of logistics sector companies in Poland in the context of macroeconomic conditions', *Scientific Papers of Silesian University of Technology Organization and Management Series*, 208, pp. 505–518. Available at: https://doi.org/10.29119/1641-3466.2024.208.29.

Pattnaik, D. *et al.* (2020) 'Trade credit research before and after the global financial crisis of 2008 – A bibliometric overview', *Research in International Business and Finance*. Netherlands: Elsevier Ltd. Available at: https://doi.org/10.1016/j.ribaf.2020.101287.

Peel, M.J., Wilson, N. and Howorth, C. (2000) 'Late payment and credit management in the small firm sector: Some empirical evidence', *International Small Business Journal*, 18(2), pp. 17–37.

Petersen, M. and Rajan, R. (1997) 'Trade credit: Theories and evidence', *Review of Financial Studies*, 10(3), pp. 661–691. Available at: https://doi.org/10.1093/rfs/10.3.661.

Philippon, T. (2016) *Fintech Opportunity*. NBER Working Paper No. w22476. Available at: https://ssrn.com/abstract=2819862 (Accessed: 22 February 2025).

Pindado, J. and Bastos, R.R. (2009) 'Trade credit, creditor protection and accounting standards: Evidence from an international sample', *Revista de economía financiera*, (17), pp. 10–33. Available at: https://www.researchgate.net/publication/228293438.

Pinto, A.P.S. *et al.* (2023) 'Bank credit and trade credit: The case of Portuguese SMEs from 2010 to 2019', *Journal of Risk and Financial Management*, 16(3). Available at: www.mdpi.com/1911-8074/16/3/170.

Pinto, J. and Costa, T. (2023) 'The impact of the ECB's PEPP on euro area bond spreads', *European Review of Business Economics*, 2(2), pp. 53–81. Available at: https://doi.org/10.26619/erbe-2022.2.2.3.

La Porta, R. *et al.* (1997) 'Legal determinants of external finance', *Journal of Finance*, 52(3), pp. 1131–1150.

La Porta, R. *et al.* (1998) 'Law and finance', *Journal of Political Economy*, 106(6), pp. 1113–1155.

Psillaki, M. and Eleftheriou, K. (2015) 'Trade credit, bank credit, and flight to quality: Evidence from French SMEs', *Journal of Small Business Management*, 53(4), pp. 1219–1240. Available at: https://doi.org/https://doi.org/10.1111/jsbm.12106.

Rahman, A., Rozsa, Z. and Cepel, M. (2018) 'Trade credit and bank finance – Evidence from the Visegrad Group', *Journal of Competitiveness*, 10(3), pp. 132–148. Available at: www.cjournal.cz/files/300.pdf.

Rajan, R.G. and Zingales, L. (1995) 'What do we know about capital structure? Some evidence from international data', *Journal of Finance*, 50(5), pp. 1421–1460.

Ramdhan, N. *et al.* (2024) 'Thriving in turbulent times: The dynamic link between economic condition and FinTech business lending success', *ASEAN Journal on Science and Technology for Development*, 41(1), pp. 110–115. Available at: https://doi.org/10.61931/2224-9028.1575.

Ross, R.A. (1977) 'The determination of financial structure. The incentive-signaling approach', *Bell Journal of Economics*, 8(1), pp. 23–40.

Salcedo-Pérez, C. and Patiño, O. (2017) 'Microfinancing and informal lending in Bogota, Colombia: A study on informal microbusinesses', *Economic Annals-XXI*, 168(11–12), pp. 57–62. Available at: https://doi.org/10.21003/ea.V168-12.

Santos, J. and Silva, A. (2014) 'The determinants of trade credit: A study of Portuguese industrial companies', *International Journal of Financial Research*, 5(4). Available at: https://doi.org/10.5430/ijfr.v5n4p128.

Sautner, Z. and Vladimirov, V. (2018) 'Indirect costs of financial distress and bankruptcy law: Evidence from trade credit and sales', *Review of Finance*, 22(5), pp. 1667–1704. Available at: https://doi.org/10.1093/rof/rfx032.

Schoenmaker, D. and Schramade, W. (2019) *Principles of Sustainable Finance*. Oxford: Oxford University Press. Available at: https://www.researchgate.net/publication/330359025.

Schwartz, R.A. (1974) 'An economic model of trade credit', *Journal of Financial and Quantitative Analysis*, 9(4), pp. 643–657. Available at: https://doi.org/10.2307/2329765.

Shi, G. (2022) 'Does industry-specific information disclosure improve trade credit financing?', *China Journal of Accounting Studies*, 10(2), pp. 203–227. Available at: https://doi.org/10.1080/21697213.2022.2086028.

Shi, X., Wang, A. and Tan, S. (2020) 'Trade-credit financing under financial constraints: A relational perspective and evidence from listed companies in China', *Emerging Markets Finance and Trade*, 56(4), pp. 860–893. Available at: https://doi.org/10.1080/1540496X.2018.1555462.

Shleifer, A. and Vishny, R.W. (1992) 'Liquidation values and debt capacity: A market equilibrium approach', *The Journal of Finance*, 47(4), pp. 1343–1366. Available at: https://doi.org/10.1111/j.1540-6261.1992.tb04661.x.

Smith, J.K. (1987) 'Trade credit and informational asymmetry', *Journal of Finance*, 42(4), pp. 863–872. Available at: https://doi.org/10.2307/2328295.

Stiglitz, J.E. and Weiss, A. (1981) 'Credit rationing in markets with imperfect information', *The American Economic Review*, 71(3), pp. 393–410. Available at: https://www.researchgate.net/publication/4733120.

Summers, B. and Wilson, N. (2000) 'Trade credit management and the decision to use factoring: An empirical study', *Journal of Business Finance & Accounting*, 27(1–2), pp. 37–68. Available at: https://doi.org/10.1111/1468-5957.00305.

Summers, B. and Wilson, N. (2003) 'Trade credit and customer relationships', *Managerial and Decision Economics*, 24(6–7), pp. 439–455. Available at: https://doi.org/10.1002/mde.1041.

Taketa, K. and Udell, G.F. (2007) 'Lending channels and financial shocks: The case of small and medium-sized enterprise trade credit and the Japanese banking crisis', *Monetary and Economic Studies,* 25(2), pp. 1–44.

Tingbani, I. *et al.* (2024) 'Trade credit and corporate growth', *International Journal of Finance and Economics*, 29(1), pp. 206–228. Available at: https://onlinelibrary.wiley.com/doi/10.1002/ijfe.2683.

Tirole, J. (2006) *The Theory of Corporate Finance*. Princeton: Princeton University Press.

Tomy, R.E. and Wittenberg-Moerman, R. (2024) 'Community membership and reciprocity in lending: Evidence from informal markets', *Journal of Accounting and Economics*, 78(1:101697). Available at: https://doi.org/10.1016/j.jacceco.2024.101697.

Trebbi, F. and Zhang, M.B. (2022) *The Cost of Regulatory Compliance in the United States*. 30691. Cambridge, MA. Available at: http://www.nber.org/papers/w30691.

Tsuruta, D. (2023) 'Bank loans, trade credit, and liquidity shortages of small businesses during the global financial crisis', *International Review of Financial Analysis*, 90, 102905. Available at: https://doi.org/10.1016/J.IRFA.2023.102905.

Uesugi, I. and Yamashiro, G. (2008) 'The relationship between trade credit and loans: Evidence from small businesses in Japan', *International Journal of Business*, 13(2), pp. 141–163. Available at: https://api.semanticscholar.org/CorpusID:37312244.

Usai, S. and Vannini, M. (2005) 'Banking structure and regional economic growth: Lessons from Italy', *Annals of Regional Science*, 39(4), pp. 691–714. Available at: https://doi.org/10.1007/s00168-005-0022-x.

Utz, R. *et al.* (2020) *Macro-Financial Implications of the COVID-19 Pandemic*. Available at: https://documents1.worldbank.org/curated/en/428531592796638957/pdf/Macro-Financial-Implications-of-the-COVID-19-Pandemic.pdf (Accessed: 7 April 2025).

Vaidya, R. (2011) 'The determinants of trade credit: Evidence from Indian manufacturing firms', *Modern Economy*, 2(5), p. 707–716.

Wang, X. *et al.* (2021) 'The financial and operational impacts of European SMEs' use of trade credit as a substitute for bank credit', *European Journal of Finance*, 27(8), pp. 796–825. Available at: https://doi.org/10.1080/1351847X.2020.1846576.

Weining, B., Jian, N. and Shubhranshu, S. (2017) 'Informal lending in emerging markets', *Marketing Science*, 37(1), pp. 123–137.

Wilner, B.S. (2000) 'The exploitation of relationships in financial distress: The case of trade credit', *Journal of Finance*, 55(1), pp. 153–178. Available at: https://doi.org/10.1111/0022-1082.00203.

Wilson, N. and Summers, B. (2002) 'Trade credit terms offered by small firms: Survey evidence and empirical analysis', *Journal of Business Finance & Accounting*, 29(3 & 4), pp. 317–351. Available at: https://doi.org/10.1111/1468-5957.00434.

Yang, S.A. and Birge, R. (2017) 'Trade credit, risk sharing, and inventory financing portfolios', *Management Science*, 64(8), pp. 3667–3689.

Yang, X. (2011) 'Trade credit versus bank credit: Evidence from corporate inventory financing', *Quarterly Review of Economics and Finance*, 51(4), pp. 419–434. Available at: https://doi.org/10.1016/j.qref.2011.07.001.

Yazdanfar, D. and Öhman, P. (2016) 'The impact of trade credit use on firm profitability: Empirical evidence from Sweden', *Journal of Advances in Management Research*, 13(2), pp. 116–129.

Yazdanfar, D. and Öhman, P. (2017) 'Substitute or complement? The use of trade credit as a financing source among SMEs', *Management Research Review*, 40(1), pp. 10–27. Available at: https://doi.org/10.1108/MRR-06-2015-0153.

Yeyati, E.L. *et al.* (2007) 'A reappraisal of state-owned banks', *Economía*, 7(2), pp. 209–259. Available at: https://about.jstor.org/terms.

Zhang, Y. (2020) 'Conditional conservatism and trade credit during the global financial crisis', *Journal of Accounting and Public Policy*, 39(4). Available at: https://doi.org/10.1016/j.jaccpubpol.2020.106728.

Zhao, L., Tang, Q. and Wang, M. (2025) 'Corporate tax credit and trade credit financing: Based on the analysis of non-public companies', *China Journal of Accounting Studies* [Preprint]. Available at: https://doi.org/10.1080/21697213.2025.2467349.

Zhou, J., Deng, L. and Gibson, P. (2020) 'SMEs' changing perspective on international trade credit risk management in China: A cultural values evolution approach', *Asia Pacific Business Review*, 28(2), pp. 1–21.

Zietek-Kwaśniewska, K. (2023) 'Cultural aspects of the use of trade credit', *Scientific Papers of Silesian University of Technology. Organization and Management Series*, 2023(182), pp. 695–711. Available at: https://doi.org/10.29119/1641-3466.2023.182.41.

2 Trade credit vs. short-term bank loan

Data and methods

2.1 Data characteristics

The primary data source for empirical research is the BACH (2023) database, i.e. the Bank for the Accounts of Companies Harmonised. This extensive dataset comprises financial data from a wide range of European companies. The development of the BACH database was a collaborative effort between the European Commission, national statistical offices and central banks. The BACH database is updated on an annual basis and is accessible to the public. It covers firms from major sectors of the economy. The main purpose of the BACH database is to standardise financial reporting for European companies and provide policymakers, researchers and stakeholders with a reliable and consistent source of financial data. It offers detailed information on company balance sheets, income statements, cash flow statements and various financial indicators. Additionally, the database includes data on company size, making it a valuable resource for analysing the performance of European companies and assessing the impact of different policies on their financial well-being.

The BACH database presents standardised annual financial data for non-financial companies in 12 EU countries. These countries include Austria (AT), Belgium (BE), the Czech Republic (CZ), Germany (DE), Spain (ES), France (FR), Croatia (HR), Italy (IT), Luxembourg (LU), Poland (PL), Portugal (PT) and Slovakia (SK). The publication of the BACH database is overseen by the European Committee of Central Balance Sheet Data Offices (ECCBSOs), which was established in 1987 and comprises a consortium of CBSOs managed by European National central banks.

DOI: 10.4324/9781003687986-2

The database comprises aggregated figures derived from income statements and balance sheets, following the respective national accounting standards. It includes individual annual accounts as well as specific financial ratios related to capital structure, debt service, profitability, activity and investment. Various measures are available for the financial report items, such as absolute values, weighted averages and quartiles. The data covers a period starting from 2000 onwards for most of the countries included in the database.

In addition to the international scope, the data in the BACH data are categorised into four size classes: small-, medium-sized enterprise and large firms. Small companies are defined as those with a turnover below 10 million euros, medium-sized companies have a turnover between 10 million euros and 50 million euros and large companies have a turnover exceeding 50 million euros. Furthermore, the database includes the industrial classification of companies based on the NACE (Nomenclature statistique des Activités économiques dans la Communauté Européenne). The NACE classification system has two levels: the first level consists of one-letter sections, while the second level comprises two-digit divisions.

Table 2.1 displays the industries included in the research, along with their corresponding three-letter symbols assigned for easier identification throughout the remainder of the study.

The expansive range of data available in the BACH database facilitates several types of comparisons. These include comparing company ratios with industry averages, comparing company ratios with those of companies within the same size category and sector, conducting mutual comparisons among different industries and performing these comparisons at various levels of data aggregation.

The study's analysis encompasses a total of 12 countries, 17 industries (classified at the section level) and 3 size classes (small, medium and large). The data are examined over a period of 21 years, specifically from 2000 to 2020. As a result, the data structure being analysed is four-dimensional and it therefore constitutes a collection of data cubes, with each cube representing a specific year. The three dimensions of the data correspond to the business sectors categorised at the section level according to the NACE classification, the size classes of firms and the countries. In total, there are 21 cubes of data analysed, with each cube representing a specific year within the analytical period of 2000 to 2020. However, it is important to note that the most recent year available for analysis as of 2023 is 2020, based

Table 2.1 Industrial sections by NACE covered by the analyses

NACE	*Section*	*Symbol*
A	Agriculture, forestry and fishing	AGR
B	Mining and quarrying	MIN
C	Manufacturing	MNF
D	Electricity, gas, steam and air conditioning supply water	ELE
E	Water supply, sewerage, waste management and remediation activities	WAT
F	Construction	CST
G	Wholesale and retail trade, repair of motor vehicles and motorcycles	TRD
H	Transportation and storage	TRS
I	Accommodation and food service activities	ACF
J	Information and communication	INF
L	Real estate activities	REA
M	Professional, scientific and technical activities	PRF
N	Administrative and support service activities	ADM
P	Education	EDU
Q	Human health and social work services	HLT
R	Arts, entertainment and recreation	ART
S	Other service activities	OSA

Source: Author's own compilation based on BACH (2023) database.

on the data release calendar. Overall, the analysed database consists of 12,852 distinct entities with four categories each, distributed as follows: 4,248 objects for each size class, 1,071 objects for each country, 756 objects for each industry and 612 objects for each year. The four dimensions defining each object available in the database provide grounds for multi-sectional analyses. The number and structure of the objects, depending on the number of dimensions included in the analysis, is shown in Table 2.2.

Certainly, not every combination of the objects' characteristics holds equal importance in terms of the research objectives. The main focus of the analyses is on four-nomial objects, i.e. size groups within countries, industries and years. Additionally, the analysis also includes more detailed comparative examinations of three-nomial objects such as:

- comparing countries within industries across size groups,
- comparing size groups within countries across industries,
- comparing size groups within industries across countries.

Table 2.2 Structure and number of objects defined by the characteristics in BACH database

One-dimensional objects		*Two-dimensional objects*		*Three-dimensional objects*		*Four-dimensional objects*	
Size groups (SIZE)	3	SIZE–CT	36	SIZE–CT–IND	612	SIZE–CT–IND–YR	12,852
Countries (CT)	12	SIZE–IND	51	SIZE–CT–YR	756		
Industries (IND)	17	CT–IND	204	CT–IND–YR	4284		
Years (YR)	21	SIZE–YR	63	IND–SIZE–YR	1071		
		CT–YR	252				
		IND–YR	357				

Source: Author's own compilation.

For each object defined by the four dimensions, several variables were computed or directly extracted from the database. The ratios utilised in this study represent ratios of means rather than means of ratios. This indicates that they were derived by averaging the balance sheet and profit and loss account data for all companies within a specific industry, country, size and year category, rather than calculating the average ratios for individual companies.

The database provides two types of data selection: variable sample and sliding sample. The variable sample encompasses all enterprises present in the database for a given year, while the sliding sample includes enterprises that appear in two consecutive years. For the purpose of this study, the sliding sample data type is employed as more suitable for economic trend analysis and cross-country comparisons.

2.2 Definition of variables

The initial step in selecting the variables for the empirical research involved reviewing previous studies that aimed to identify the factors influencing corporate trade credit. This review revealed several diagnostic variables that were frequently utilised in research on trade credit behaviour and were considered significant.

There are two primary rationales for employing these commonly used variables. First, these ratios have been extensively tested and carefully considered, ensuring their measurement is reliable. Second, by using popular ratios instead of unique or unconventional ones, the research results can be easily compared with earlier findings. Additionally, the availability and reliability of data play a crucial role in ensuring the analysis is justifiable.

For each object defined by the four or fewer dimensions described in the previous section, a set of dependent and explanatory variables was calculated. Regarding the dependent variables, three measures of trade credit were employed to capture essential aspects of trade credit behaviour. Net trade credit was used to represent the overall trade credit position of a firm, calculated as the difference between accounts receivable and accounts payable relative to total assets. Trade credit provided, which is obtained by scaling accounts receivable by total assets, measures the extent to which a company extends credit to its customers. Additionally, trade credit obtained, determined by the ratio of accounts payable to assets, reflects the firm's reliance on trade credit from its suppliers. These variables provide insights into different dimensions of trade credit relationships. Table 2.3 provides a detailed breakdown of the construction of these ratios.

These variables, widely used in earlier research on trade credit, have been well-established and validated in the existing literature. The formulas for the variables are straightforward and easy to compute using commonly available financial data. This simplicity allows for consistent measurement across firms and facilitates comparability across studies. Moreover, the ratios offer meaningful interpretations. Net trade credit provides a measure of a firm's net exposure to trade credit, while trade credit provided and obtained offers insights into

Table 2.3 Dependent variables

Symbol	*Ratio definition*	*Literature reference*
NTC	Net trade credit = (Accounts receivable – Accounts payable)/Assets	Lin and Chou (2015); Madaleno, Bărbuţă-Mişu and Deari (2019) McGuinness, Hogan and Powell (2018)
REC	Trade credit provided = Accounts receivable/Assets	Lin and Chou (2015); McGuinness, Hogan and Powell (2018)
PAY	Trade credit obtained = Accounts payable/Assets	Lin and Chou (2015); McGuinness, Hogan and Powell (2018)

Source: Author's own compilation.

the firm's credit policies and reliance on supplier credit. Finally, the use of commonly employed variables enhances comparability with earlier research. In summary, the choice of measures of trade credit is justified due to their conceptual relevance, acceptance in prior literature, simplicity of calculation, interpretability and comparability with previous studies.

Similarly, the selection of explanatory variables listed in Table 2.4 aligns with the factors typically examined as the primary determinants of trade credit policy by other studies in the field. The selected variables are grounded in theoretical frameworks and prior research on trade credit determinants. They capture different dimensions of a firm's financial health, operational efficiency, country, size, industry affiliation and temporal effects. These factors are conceptually linked to trade credit decisions and are known to affect a firm's willingness and ability to extend or obtain trade credit. The selected explanatory variables are commonly available financial metrics or categorical variables. The use of dummy variables such as size classes, countries, industries and years allows for comparative analysis across different groups and periods. This facilitates the identification of variations in trade credit determinants across firms of different sizes, countries, industries and over time.

In summary, the inclusion of the above-listed explanatory variables as determinants of trade credit is justified based on their theoretical foundations, empirical evidence supporting their relevance, data availability, conceptual alignment with trade credit decisions and the opportunity for comparative analysis.

2.3 Hypotheses' development

Drawing from existing knowledge and research in the field (e.g. Andrieu, Staglianò and Zwan, 2018), it is generally believed that trade credit and short-term bank loans have a complementary effect rather than a substitution effect. However, several studies, including Pinto *et al.* (2023) or Palacín-Sánchez, Canto-Cuevas and Di-Pietro (2019), support the substitution hypothesis. The conflicting empirical results create an opportunity to explore the reasons behind these contradictory findings. One possible explanation is that the relationship between trade credit and short-term bank financing is contingent upon other factors. Country-specific conditions, industrial characteristics and firm size-related attributes may not only directly impact trade

Table 2.4 Explanatory variables

Variable character	*Symbol*	*Ratio definition*	*Literature reference*
Firm-specific financial ratios	BKL	Short-term bank loan = Current amounts owed to credit institutions/ Assets	Lin and Chou (2015); Lawrenz and Oberndorfer (2018); McGuinness, Hogan and Powell (2018); (Białek-Jaworska and Nehrebecka (2016)
	COL	Collateral = Fixed assets/Assets	Lawrenz and Oberndorfer (2018); McGuinness, Hogan and Powell (2018); Białek-Jaworska and Nehrebecka (2016); Pinto, Henriques, da Silva Cardoso, *et al.* (2023); Yang (2011a)
	INV	Inventory = Inventories/Assets	Lin and Chou (2015); Białek-Jaworska and Nehrebecka (2016)
	CSH	Cash at hand = Cash and available bank amounts/Assets	Lawrenz and Oberndorfer (2018); McGuinness, Hogan and Powell (2018)
	CGS	Costs of goods sold = Costs of goods sold, materials and consumables/Net turnover	Lin and Chou (2015)
	DBT	Debt ratio = Debt/Equity	Lawrenz and Oberndorfer (2018)
	ROA	Return on assets = Net operating profit/ Assets	Lawrenz and Oberndorfer (2018); Carvalho and Schiozer (2015); Pinto, Henriques, da Silva Cardoso, *et al.* (2023)
	TAT	Total asset turnover = Net turnover/Assets	Lin and Chou (2015); García-Teruel and Martínez-Solano (2010)

Table 2.4 (Continued)

Variable character	*Symbol*	*Ratio definition*	*Literature reference*
Dummy variables	SIZE	Size groups of firms (S, M, L)	Andrieu, Staglianò and Zwan (2018); Palacín-Sánchez, Canto-Cuevas and Di-Pietro (2019)
	CT	Countries (AT, BE, CZ, DE, ES, FR, HR, IT, LU, PL, PT, SK)	Andrieu, Staglianò and Zwan (2018)
	IND	Industries (AGR, MIN, MNF, ELE, WAT, CST, TRD, TRS, ACF, INF, REA, PRF, ADM, EDU, HLT, ART, OSA)	Andrieu, Staglianò and Zwan (2018)
	YEAR	Years (2000, …, 2020)	Andrieu, Staglianò and Zwan (2018)

Source: Author's own compilation.

credit policies but also indirectly influence the relationship between trade credit and bank loans.

One of the reasons supporting the idea of a complementary relationship is that trade credit and short-term bank loans often serve different financing purposes. Trade credit is primarily used for transactional purposes, such as purchasing goods or services from suppliers, while short-term bank loans are typically obtained to cover broader working capital needs. Firms may utilise both sources concurrently to meet their financing requirements, making use of the strengths of each source for different aspects of their operations.

Second, accessing multiple financing sources can help firms diversify their funding and reduce risk. By relying on both trade credit and short-term bank loans, firms can spread their financial obligations across multiple providers, reducing their dependence on a single source of financing. This diversification can enhance financial stability and mitigate the risk of disruptions in the event of changes in credit terms, supplier insolvency or difficulties in obtaining bank loans.

Moreover, the combination of trade credit and short-term bank loans offers firms flexibility and adaptability in managing their cash flow and working capital. Trade credit provides a flexible means of financing that adjusts to the firm's transactional needs and the credit terms offered by suppliers. Short-term bank loans, on the other hand, offer greater control over the timing and amount of funding, allowing firms to address short-term liquidity needs and take advantage of investment opportunities.

Another reason pertains to synergistic effects of trade credit and short-term bank loans, which can complement each other in terms of their impact on financial performance. For example, trade credit may help improve a firm's liquidity position by extending payment terms, while bank loans can provide additional funds for growth initiatives or investment projects. The combined use of these financing sources can enable firms to achieve better overall financial performance than relying on a single source alone.

Finally, by utilising trade credit, firms can build and strengthen their relationships with suppliers, potentially leading to preferential treatment, discounts or improved terms. Access to short-term bank loans can also support these relationships by ensuring timely payments and demonstrating financial stability.

Summarising, the prevailing view suggests that a complementary relationship is more likely due to the unique and complementary benefits that each financing source offers. This leads to formulating the following research hypothesis:

H1: Trade credit and short-term bank loans are complementary.

It is important to consider that the relationship between trade credit and short-term bank loans may differ depending on various factors such as industries, firm characteristics and economic conditions. Therefore, the hypothesis will be tested not only for the entire sample, but also for different size groups, countries and industries. Additionally, since there are three measures of trade credit being examined, the H1 hypothesis can be divided into three corresponding hypotheses:

- H1a: There is a positive relation between net trade credit and short-term bank loan.
- H1b: There is a positive relation between trade credit offered and short-term bank loan.
- H1c: There is a positive relation between trade credit obtained and short-term bank loan.

Another set of research hypotheses pertains to the relative significance of the three effects that are the primary focal point in terms of their relevance to the behaviour of corporate trade credit. These effects include the country effect, industry effect and firm size effect. Consequently, the hypotheses H2–H4 can be formulated as follows:

H2: The industry effect has a greater significance than the country effect in terms of trade credit.
H3: The industry effect has a greater significance than the firm size effect in terms of trade credit.
H4: The firm size effect has a greater significance than the country effect in terms of trade credit.

By analogy to H1, hypotheses H2–H4 should also be decomposed into three sub-hypotheses each, regarding the three trade credit measures. For this purpose, the same letter extensions a–c are used to indicate which specific trade credit measures are being addressed: (a) for net trade credit, (b) for trade credit granted and (c) for trade credit received.

The prevalence of industry effect over country effect in trade credit – reflected in the **H2** – can be supported among others by industry-specific risk. Trade credit decisions are influenced by the risk factors associated with the industry in which the buyer and seller operate. Industries have unique characteristics, such as demand volatility, supply chain complexities and competitive dynamics. These factors significantly impact creditworthiness and payment behaviour within the industry, making industry effects more influential than country effects. Another argument in favour of the H2 refers to the supplier-specific knowledge. Suppliers often possess extensive knowledge about the specific industries they serve, as well as a deeper understanding of industry dynamics, customer behaviour and creditworthiness within their sector. Consequently, suppliers are more likely to assess credit risk based on industry-specific factors rather than general country-level considerations.

Moreover, industries often form tight-knit trade credit networks, where businesses interact and build relationships with their industry counterparts. These networks foster trust, information sharing and common credit practices within the industry. As a result, trade credit decisions tend to align with the norms and practices of the specific industry, emphasising the industry effect over the country effect. The contractual nature of trade credit involves negotiated terms between suppliers and buyers, often influenced by industry norms and legal frameworks (Klapper, Laeven and Rajan, 2012).

Furthermore, industries may have unique regulatory frameworks or industry-specific payment terms that influence trade credit decisions. For instance, certain industries may have established standard payment periods, credit insurance practices or industry-specific payment guarantees. These factors further highlight the dominance of industry-specific considerations in trade credit.

Additionally, companies operating within the same industry tend to exhibit comparable creditworthiness characteristics due to shared market conditions, customer bases and operational factors. This similarity in credit profiles provides a logical basis for suppliers to assess credit risk primarily based on industry-specific factors rather than relying solely on general country-level indicators. By considering the creditworthiness patterns within an industry, suppliers can make more informed trade credit decisions.

Similarly, assessing the financial health and creditworthiness of businesses within a specific industry requires a focus on industry-specific performance indicators. Metrics like production volumes, sales growth and inventory turnover provide valuable insights into the industry's overall performance. Suppliers are more likely to rely on these industry-specific indicators rather than broader country-level economic indicators when evaluating trade credit options. By utilising industry performance indicators, suppliers can gain a more accurate understanding of the creditworthiness of buyers within their respective industries.

Finally, different industries often exhibit distinct trade practices and payment terms that are prevalent within their sector. For example, industries such as fashion or electronics commonly engage in consignment sales, require advance payments or offer instalment-based credit terms. These industry-specific trade practices further emphasise the importance of industry effects in trade credit. Suppliers operating within these industries need to adapt their credit terms and practices to align with the specific trade norms and preferences of their industry. Understanding and accommodating industry-specific trade practices enhances the effectiveness and relevance of trade credit decisions.

To sum up, considering similar creditworthiness patterns, industry performance indicators and industry-specific trade practices collectively highlight the prevalence of industry effects over country effects in trade credit. By focusing on industry-specific factors, suppliers can better assess credit risk, adjust their credit terms and make more informed decisions when extending trade credit within a particular industry.

That the impact of the specific industry in which a firm operates on its trade credit practices is greater than the influence of a firm's size on its trade credit decisions – as hypothesised in **H3** – might be less obvious. While the firm size effect is undoubtedly relevant in trade credit decisions, the industry effect covers a wider range of factors that shape trade credit practices within an industry.

First, the industry effect plays a crucial role in shaping trade credit behaviour by determining the market dynamics and competitiveness within an industry. Different industries have unique characteristics, such as the level of competition, the nature of products or services and the financial stability of customers and suppliers. These factors directly influence trade credit practices, including credit terms, payment periods and credit limits.

Furthermore, certain industries inherently carry more risks than others due to factors such as regulatory constraints, technological disruptions or fluctuating demand. These industry-specific risks have a direct impact on the creditworthiness and financial stability of firms within the industry. Consequently, trade credit decisions, such as the extension of credit terms and limits, are often influenced by the perceived risk levels associated with the industry, making the industry effect significant in trade credit risk assessment and management practices.

Moreover, the dynamics within supplier and customer relationships vary across industries, affecting trade credit decisions. Some industries witness suppliers with significant bargaining power, allowing them to dictate trade credit terms, while others involve customers with more leverage to negotiate favourable trade credit terms. Understanding the industry-specific power dynamics and relationships is crucial for effective trade credit management, emphasising the greater influence of the industry effect on trade credit practices.

Additionally, industries often differ in terms of norms, practices and standards regarding trade credit, which heavily shape the trade credit policies adopted by firms within that industry. For instance, in industries where trade credit is common, firms may offer more lenient credit terms to remain competitive. Conversely, industries with limited trade credit practices may witness firms adopting stricter credit policies. Consequently, the industry effect heavily influences trade credit decisions by setting industry-specific benchmarks and norms.

Lastly, the industry effect takes into account the broader economic and market conditions that impact trade credit practices. Economic factors like interest rates, inflation rates and overall market stability significantly influence the availability and cost of credit for firms. Industries that are highly sensitive to economic fluctuations often adjust their trade credit policies accordingly to mitigate financial risks. Thus, the industry effect assumes greater significance in managing and responding to macroeconomic factors that affect trade credit.

In summary, the industry effect plays a crucial role in trade credit practices by shaping market dynamics, influencing risk assessment, determining power dynamics in supplier and customer relationships, establishing industry norms and practices and responding to economic and market conditions. The unique characteristics, risks, relationships and practices specific to each industry make the industry effect more significant in determining trade credit policies and behaviours.

According to **H4**, the significance of the firm size effect in trade credit decisions outweighs the influence of the country effect. One key advantage of the firm size effect is the flexibility and customisation it offers. Smaller firms often have more personalised relationships with suppliers and customers, enabling them to negotiate favourable credit terms that suit their specific needs and circumstances. In contrast, the country effect tends to impose more standardised regulations and policies that apply to all firms, irrespective of their size, limiting the ability to tailor trade credit arrangements.

Moreover, the access to financing differs between large and small firms, further highlighting the importance of the firm size effect. Larger firms generally have better access to financing options such as bank loans or equity financing. Consequently, they may rely less on trade credit as a source of financing. In contrast, smaller firms heavily rely on trade credit due to limited access to alternative forms of capital. This discrepancy emphasises the significance of the firm size effect in determining trade credit practices.

Market power also plays a crucial role in trade credit decisions. Larger firms possess greater market power, which enables them to negotiate more favourable credit terms. They can take advantage of their size and influence to secure longer payment periods or lower interest rates. Smaller firms, lacking the same bargaining power, may be subject to less favourable credit conditions. As a result, the firm size effect becomes more pronounced in influencing trade credit outcomes.

Lastly, as globalisation and market integration continue to advance, trade credit decisions are increasingly influenced by global market factors rather than country-specific factors. Firms of all sizes engage in cross-border trade, forming international supply chains and dealing with customers and suppliers from various countries. Consequently, the firm size effect is likely to become more significant as firms cope with the complexities of global trade, regardless of the in country in which they are based.

The last set of research hypotheses focuses on examining the varying effects of explanatory variables on trade credit measures. The aim is to investigate the dissimilarities in how different factors impact corporate policies in the field of trade credit. Hypotheses H5–H7 can provide insights into understanding the relationships between explanatory variables and trade credit. They are formulated as follows:

H5: The significance and direction of the impact of explanatory variables on trade credit differs across size groups of firms.
H6: The significance and direction of the impact of explanatory variables on trade credit differs across countries.
H7: The significance and direction of the impact of explanatory variables on trade credit differs across industries.

By analogy to hypothesis H1, which can be verified with respect to the three trade credit measures, hypotheses H5–H7 are similarly decomposed into more detailed statements. Consequently, H5 consists of:

- H5a: The significance and direction of the impact of explanatory variables on net trade credit differs across size groups of firms.
- H5b: The significance and direction of the impact of explanatory variables on trade credit offered differs across size groups of firms.
- H5c: The significance and direction of the impact of explanatory variables on trade credit obtained differs across size groups of firms.

The hypotheses H6 and H7 are broken down analogically.

Naturally, the occurrence of similarities or dissimilarities in the impact of explanatory variables on trade credit measures is likely to vary depending on each individual variable. Consequently, it is possible to test each of the hypotheses H5–H7 with respect to the specific explanatory variables utilised in the analysis. This could potentially lead to further breakdown of the hypotheses into more detailed specifications. However, for the sake of clarity, the more detailed specification will not be implemented in this case. Nevertheless, the verification of the hypotheses will still be conducted as comprehensively as possible, considering the variables that are employed.

The verification of the hypotheses H5–H7 was based on the similarity analysis of the impact of variables on trade credit measures between:

- size classes of firms,
- countries,
- industrial sections.

The following procedure was applied in order to evaluate the similarity of impact. The impact was considered as similar if the relationship between an explanatory variable and trade credit measure was either:

- significantly positive for the two compared categories (size classes, countries or industries),
- significantly negative for the two compared categories,
- insignificant for the two compared categories.

The impact was considered as different if the relationship between an explanatory variable and trade credit measure was either:

- significantly positive for one category and significantly negative for the other of the two compared categories (size classes, countries or industries),
- significantly positive for one category and insignificant for the other of two compared categories,
- significantly negative for one category and insignificant for the other of two compared categories.

The pairwise comparisons were made for each of the three dependent variables separately, i.e. between each explanatory variable (including dummy variables) and net trade credit, between each explanatory variable and accounts receivable ratio and between each explanatory variable and accounts payable ratio. Then, for each explanatory variable, the share of similar relationships was determined. This provided grounds for identifying the stable variables, i.e. the ones which demonstrate high similarity indexes across compared categories, as well as the varying factors, i.e. the variables with lower similarity indexes.

2.4 Research methods

The study employed methods that are consistent with the primary research objectives, i.e. to determine whether trade credit and short-term bank loans serve as complementary or substitutable sources of corporate short-term financing, on the one hand, and, on the other hand, to identify the relative importance of country, industry and firm size as determinants of corporate short-term financing decisions. The analysis is conducted not only for the entire dataset but also for various size categories of companies, across different countries and industries, considering the data's structure.

The initial stage of the research process focused on identifying the level and variation of trade credit measures and their underlying factors. To achieve this, descriptive statistics were analysed across three sections: countries, industries and firm size classes. The results of this analysis can be found in subchapter 3.1, providing a summary of the findings. Following the preliminary descriptive analysis, a correlation analysis was conducted for the entire dataset, as well as separately within the aforementioned sections.

The data structure, which is a combination of cross-sectional data and time series, implies the use of the panel data approach to explore the relation between trade credit and bank credit, as well as other factors. This constitutes the next and the main part of the empirical analysis in this study. When applying panel data modelling, several alternative approaches should be considered (Gostkowska-Drzewicka and Majerowska, 2019). The first and, at the same time, the simplest method is the pooled model, called a restricted one, which assumes that all individual units are homogeneous. As a result, the structural parameters of the model are the same for all units in all periods, whereas the differences between empirical and theoretical values of the exogenous variable result only from the disturbances, whose distribution is the same for each unit. According to the second method, i.e. the fixed effects (FE) model assumption, the individual-specific effects are correlated with the independent variables. Thus, every individual unit has its own specific part of variability, although no specific effects for time periods are observed. Finally, the last approach, the random effects (REs) model, assumes that the individual-specific effects are uncorrelated with the independent variable. Therefore, each of the individual effects is a part of the stochastic disturbance, i.e. the error term.

The verification of research hypotheses specified in the previous subchapter relies on conducting panel data regression analyses. These regressions are performed for the entire dataset and subsequently for each size class, country and industry separately. The most comprehensive version of the model can be represented by formula (2.1):

$$\begin{aligned} TC_{cist} = {} & \beta_0 + \beta_1 BKL_{cist} + \beta_2 COL_{cist} + \beta_3 INV_{cist} + \beta_4 CSH_{cist} \\ & + \beta_5 CGS_{cist} + + \beta_6 DBT_{cist} + \beta_7 ROA_{cist} + \beta_8 TAT_{cist} \\ & + \beta_9 SIZE_s + \beta_{10} CT_c + \beta_{11} \gamma_i IND_i + + \beta_{12} YEAR_t + \xi_{cist}, \end{aligned} \tag{2.1}$$

where:

- TC_{cist} denotes one of the three trade credit measures (NTC_{cist} – net trade credit, i.e. the difference between accounts receivable and payable scaled by total assets, REC_{cist} – trade credit given represented by accounts receivable to total assets, PAY_{cist} – trade credit obtained represented by accounts payable to total assets) for country *c*, industry *i*, firm size *s* in year *t*,
- BKL_{cist} is the short-term bank loan, i.e. current amounts owed to credit institutions to total assets,
- COL_{cist} is the relation of fixed to total assets,
- INV_{cist} are the inventories to total balance sheet,
- CSH_{cist} is the cash and available bank amounts to assets,
- CGS_{cist} are the costs of goods sold, materials and consumables to net turnover,
- DBT_{cist} is the liabilities to equity ratio,
- TAT_{cist} is the total assets turnover, i.e. the relation of sales to assets,
- $SIZE_s$ correspond to size groups of firms (S, M, L), *s=3*,
- CT_c represent dummy variables for each country (AT, BE, CZ, DE, ES, FR, HR, IT, LU, PL, PT, SK), *c=12*,

- IND_i represent dummy variables for industries (AGR, MIN, MNF, ELE, WAT, CST, TRD, TRS, ACF, INF, REA, PRF, ADM, EDU, HLT, ART, OSA), $i=17$,
- $YEAR_t$ is a set of year dummy variables (2000, …, 2020), $t=21$,
- $\beta_{1\text{-}12}$ are structural parameters,
- ξ is the random error.

Given that there are three distinct dependent variables, the model has been divided into three corresponding variations: (2.1.a) pertains to net trade credit as the dependent variable, (2.1.b) focuses on trade credit offered and (2.1.c) centres on trade credit received. The letter extensions applied to the model numbers align with the numbering and symbols of the hypotheses. This approach is adopted to systematically explore the impacts of various independent variables on each of the three dependent variables. This structured approach facilitates a comprehensive examination of different aspects of the relationship between the independent and dependent variables.

Initially, the models (2.1.a)–(2.1.c) were estimated using pooled ordinary least squares (OLS) without any dummy variables. This estimation was conducted for the entire dataset, with a different dependent variable representing various trade credit measures each time. Insignificant variables were then sequentially removed from the model. Panel specification tests were subsequently performed to determine the most appropriate model for explaining the dependent variable.

According to the methodological procedure, the appropriateness of the pooled OLS model is first tested using the joint significance test. The null hypothesis of the test assumes that the pooled OLS panel model is appropriate, while the alternative hypothesis suggests that the REs model is more suitable (Majerowska and Gostkowska-Drzewicka, 2021). The next step aims to verify whether individual effects exist and, if so, to identify which is the most accurate model to estimate them. The Lagrange Multiplier test by Breusch and Pagan (1980) is used to identify the existence of individual effects. If the null hypothesis of no unobserved heterogeneity is rejected, a model capturing individual heterogeneity is considered appropriate. Thus, it is first necessary to determine if there is a correlation between the unobservable heterogeneity of each object and the explanatory variables of the model. In the case of a correlation (FE), the consistent estimation would be obtained by the within-group estimator. If there is no correlation (RE), a more efficient estimator is obtained by estimating the equation in levels by generalised least squares. The usual strategy for the specification of the fixed versus random nature of the effects is to use the Hausman (1978) test under the null hypothesis that the RE model is consistent and efficient, implying that the individual-specific effects are not correlated with the explanatory variables. If the null hypothesis is rejected, the effects are considered to be fixed, indicating that the individual-specific effects are correlated with the explanatory variables and the estimation of the model is carried out by OLS. If the null hypothesis is accepted, this suggests that using a RE model is justified, implying that the unobserved individual-specific effects are assumed to be uncorrelated with the explanatory variables and can be modelled as random (García-Teruel and Martínez-Solano, 2010).

In the majority of cases, the FE model demonstrated suitability. In such situations, the model (2.1) was recalculated by including all dummy variables. Subsequently, a Wald test was conducted for each group of dummy variables, namely size, country, industry and year, to assess the overall significance of each variable category. If the panel specification tests confirmed the suitability of the RE model, interpretations were made based on this particular version of the model.

The subsequent stage involved estimating the adjusted model (2.1) separately for each size group. In this case, the adjustment involved removing the size dummy variables from the model, resulting in a simplified equation, referred to as (2.2):

$$\begin{aligned} TC_{cist} = {} & \beta_0 + \beta_1 BKL_{cist} + \beta_2 COL_{cist} + \beta_3 INV_{cist} + \beta_4 CSH_{cist} \\ & + \beta_5 CGS_{cist} + + \beta_6 DBT_{cist} + \beta_7 ROA_{cist} + \beta_8 TAT_{cist} \\ & + \beta_9 CT_c + \beta_{10} \gamma_i IND_i + \beta_{11} YEAR_t + \xi_{cist},, \end{aligned} \tag{2.2}$$

Similar to the extended model estimated for the entire dataset, three variations of model (2.2) were estimated for various trade credit measures: (2.2.a) for net trade credit (NTC_{cist}) as the dependent variable, (2.2.b) for trade credit offered (REC_{cist}) and (2.2.c) for trade credit received (PAY_{cist}). Estimating models (2.2.a)–(2.2.c) for each specific size class serves the purpose of not only comparing the direction and significance of key determinants of trade credit but also assessing the relative significance of the country and industry effects across different size groups of firms.

Subsequently, the adjusted model (2.1) was estimated separately for each country. In this case, the modification involved removing the country dummy variables from the model, resulting in a reduced equation, referred to as (2.3):

$$\begin{aligned} TC_{cist} = {} & \beta_0 + \beta_1 BKL_{cist} + \beta_2 COL_{cist} + \beta_3 INV_{cist} + \beta_4 CSH_{cist} \\ & + \beta_5 CGS_{cist} + +\beta_6 DBT_{cist} + \beta_7 ROA_{cist} + \beta_8 TAT_{cist} \\ & + \sum_{s=1}^{3} \gamma_s SIZE + \sum_{i=1}^{17} \gamma_i IND + + \sum_{t=1}^{21} \gamma_t YEAR + \xi_{cist}, \end{aligned} \tag{2.3}$$

Once again, three variations of model (2.3) were estimated using different trade credit measures: (2.3.a)–(2.3.c), following the same methodology applied to the entire dataset. Estimating models (2.3.a)–(2.3.c) for each individual country enables a comparison of the significance of trade credit determinants among European economies, as well as an assessment of the relative importance of the industry and size effects across countries.

Finally, the last modification made to the initial model (2.1) aimed to customise it for estimation across different industrial sectors. This was achieved by excluding the industry dummy variables from the original version, resulting in the following equation (2.4) representing the model for individual industries:

$$\begin{aligned} TC_{cist} = {} & \beta_0 + \beta_1 BKL_{cist} + \beta_2 COL_{cist} + \beta_3 INV_{cist} + \beta_4 CSH_{cist} \\ & + \beta_5 CGS_{cist} + +\beta_6 DBT_{cist} + \beta_7 ROA_{cist} + \beta_8 TAT_{cist} \\ & + \sum_{s=1}^{3} \gamma_s SIZE + \sum_{c=1}^{12} \gamma_c CT + + \sum_{t=1}^{21} \gamma_t YEAR + \xi_{cist}, \end{aligned} \tag{2.4}$$

Again, the letter extensions a–c added to the model number (2.4) correspond to the three trade credit dependent variables. All variations of the models (2.1–2.4) were estimated using the Arellano robustness test to account for heteroscedasticity and autocorrelation.

To summarise, the comprehensive model (2.1) with the highest number of dummy variables was applied to the entire population, which consisted of four-nomial objects including groups of firms

Table 2.5 Variable inclusion in models estimated for various object groups

Variable character and symbol (model extension)			*Model description by number of the formula and objects included as groups of firms in:*											
			(2.1)			*(2.2)*			*(2.3)*			*(2.4)*		
			Countries, industries, size groups			*Countries, industries*			*Industries, size groups*			*Countries, size groups*		
	Dependent	(a) NTC	•			•			•			•		
		(b) REC		•			•			•			•	
		(c) PAY			•			•			•			•
Independent	**Firm-specific variables**	BKL	•	•	•	•	•	•	•	•	•	•	•	•
		COL	•	•	•	•	•	•	•	•	•	•	•	•
		INV	•	•	•	•	•	•	•	•	•	•	•	•
		CSH	•	•	•	•	•	•	•	•	•	•	•	•
		CGS	•	•	•	•	•	•	•	•	•	•	•	•
		DBT	•	•	•	•	•	•	•	•	•	•	•	•
		ROA	•	•	•	•	•	•	•	•	•	•	•	•
		TAT	•	•	•	•	•	•	•	•	•	•	•	•
	Dummy variables	SIZE	•	•	•				•	•	•	•	•	•
		CT	•	•	•	•	•	•				•	•	•
		IND	•	•	•	•	•	•	•	•	•			
		YEAR	•	•	•	•	•	•	•	•	•	•	•	•

Source: Author's own compilation.

Note: • indicates the variable inclusion in the model.

categorised by size classes, countries, industries and years. The modified versions of the initial model, namely models (2.2)–(2.4), were estimated for three-nomial objects as follows:

- groups of firms categorised by countries, industries and years – for each size class;
- groups of firms categorised by industries, size classes and years – for each country;
- groups of firms categorised by countries, size classes and years – for each industry.

Table 2.5 provides a summary of the variables included in each model version for convenient reference.

The models (2.2)–(2.4) allow for the identification of the indirect influence of excluded variables on trade credit through cross-sectional comparisons. These comparisons can be made:

- across size groups, to determine the indirect impact of firm size on trade credit.
- across countries, to determine the indirect impact of country-specific factors on trade credit.
- across industrial sectors, to determine the indirect impact of industry-specific factors on trade credit.

This multi-sectional approach provides a framework for drawing dual-layered conclusions regarding both direct and indirect factors that contribute to corporate trade credit policies.

References

Andrieu, G., Staglianò, R. and Zwan, P. van der (2018) 'Bank debt and trade credit for SMEs in Europe: firm-, industry-, and country-level determinants', *Small Business Economics*, 51, pp. 245–264. Available at: https://doi.org/10.1007/s11187-017-9926-y.

BACH (2023) *Bank for the Accounts of Companies Harmonized*. Banque de France, www.bach.banque-france.fr

Breusch, T.S. and Pagan, A.R. (1980) 'The Lagrange multiplier test and its applications to model specification in econometrics', *The Review of Economic Studies*, 47(1), pp. 239–253. Available at: https://doi.org/https://doi.org/10.2307/2297111.

García-Teruel, P.J. and Martínez-Solano, P. (2010) 'Determinants of trade credit: A comparative study of European SMEs', *International Small Business Journal*, 28(3), pp. 215–233. Available at: https://doi.org/10.1177/0266242609360603.

Gostkowska-Drzewicka, M. and Majerowska, E. (2019) 'Determinants of corporate dividend policy in Polish companies listed on WSE', *e-Finanse*, 15(3), pp. 47–55. Available at: https://doi.org/10.2478/fiqf-2019-0019.

Hausman, J.A. (1978) 'Specification tests in econometrics', *Econometrica*, 46(6), pp. 1251–1271 (. Available at: https://doi.org/https://doi.org/10.2307/1913827.

Klapper, L., Laeven, L. and Rajan, R. (2012) 'Trade credit contracts', *Review of Financial Studies*, 25(3), pp. 838–867. Available at: https://doi.org/10.1093/rfs/hhr122.

Lawrenz, J., and Oberndorfer, J. (2018) 'Firm size effects in trade credit supply and demand', *Journal of Banking and Finance*, 93, pp. 1–20. https://doi.org/10.1016/j.jbankfin.2018.05.014

Majerowska, E. and Gostkowska-Drzewicka, M. (2021) *Czynniki struktury kapitału oraz rentowności spółek giełdowych. Ujęcie teoretyczne i empiryczne*. Gdańsk: Wydawnictwo Uniwersytetu Gdańskiego.

Palacín-Sánchez, M., Canto-Cuevas, F. and Di-Pietro, F. (2019) 'Trade credit versus bank credit: A simultaneous analysis in European SMEs', *Small Business Economics*, 53(4), pp. 1079–1096. Available at: https://doi.org/10.1007/s11187-018-0101-x.

Pinto, A.P.S. *et al.* (2023) 'Bank credit and trade credit: The case of Portuguese SMEs from 2010 to 2019', *Journal of Risk and Financial Management*, 16, pp. 1–19. Available at: www.mdpi.com/1911-8074/16/3/170.

3 Corporate short-term financing in Europe

A study of European companies

3.1 Descriptive statistics of corporate short-term finance behaviour

The first cross-section considered in this study relates to firm size. The mean values of all dependent and firm-specific explanatory variables across size groups are presented in Table 3.1. The mean values represent all countries, industries and years included in the study.

Additionally, the mean values of the dependent variables across size classes are shown in Figure 3.1 visualising the average levels of these variables and their variations among businesses of different sizes.

The analysis of net trade credit (NTC) reveals notable differences across firm sizes: small businesses exhibit the highest mean NTC and grant more trade credit on average, while medium and large businesses show lower values, though trade credit obtained (PAY) is relatively similar across size classes. Examination of the dependent variables in Table 3.1 highlights further patterns: smaller firms rely less on short-term bank loans, while medium-sized firms use more collateral relative to assets; inventory management practices are consistent across sizes. Cash holdings are comparable for small and medium firms but slightly lower for large firms. Cost ratios vary, with larger firms showing lower costs relative to net turnover. Debt ratios increase with firm size, while return on assets is lower for small firms and highest for medium-sized firms. Total asset turnover is also highest for medium-sized businesses, suggesting greater efficiency in generating turnover relative to assets. Overall, the findings reveal the distinct financial profiles and credit behaviours of firms by size.

In this study, the second cross-section analysed is the international cross-section. Table 3.2 displays the average values of the dependent

DOI: 10.4324/9781003687986-3

Table 3.1 Mean values of variables across size classes

Size	*Dependent variables*			*Explanatory firm-specific variables*							
	NTC	*REC*	*PAY*	*BKL*	*COL*	*INV*	*CSH*	*CGS*	*DBT*	*ROA*	*TAT*
SMALL	0.038	0.173	0.135	0.060	0.524	0.077	0.077	0.325	0.645	0.031	0.765
MEDIUM	0.023	0.142	0.120	0.069	0.567	0.074	0.075	0.335	0.643	0.048	0.897
LARGE	0.036	0.157	0.121	0.035	0.526	0.076	0.071	0.286	0.663	0.042	0.840

Source: Author's calculations based on BACH (2023).

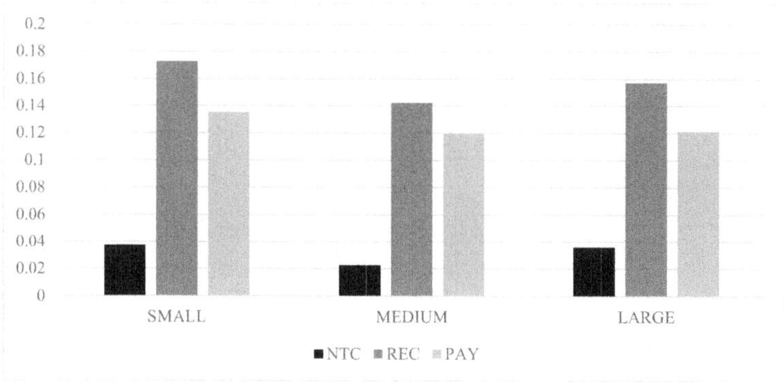

Figure 3.1 Mean values of trade credit ratios across size classes.

and firm-specific explanatory variables for individual countries. These mean values encompass all size categories, industries and years considered within the study.

Figure 3.2 illustrates the mean values of the dependent variables across countries, revealing several patterns. NTC is highest in Austria, Croatia, Italy and Luxembourg, while Belgium, the Czech Republic, France and Slovakia show lower values. Poland stands out with the highest mean for both trade credit granted and obtained, with Austria, Croatia, Portugal and Spain also displaying elevated values, whereas Belgium, the Czech Republic, France and Slovakia again show lower means. In contrast, explanatory variables such as short-term bank loans, collateral, inventory levels, cash holdings, cost structures, debt ratios, return on assets and total asset turnover exhibit relatively minor variation across countries, indicating broadly similar financial characteristics among firms regardless of location. Overall, the analysis reveals moderate cross-country differences in trade credit use but general consistency in firms' financial structures.

The final key aspect examined in this research focuses on the industrial cross-section of companies. Table 3.3 illustrates the average values of the dependent and firm-specific explanatory variables for individual industries. These average values encompass all size categories, countries and years included in the study.

Moreover, Figure 3.3 displays the average values of the dependent variables being analysed across different industries. This visual

Table 3.2 Mean values of variables across countries

Country	*Dependent variables*			*Explanatory firm-specific variables*							
	NTC	*REC*	*PAY*	*BKL*	*COL*	*INV*	*CSH*	*CGS*	*DBT*	*ROA*	*TAT*
AT	0.035	0.157	0.122	0.052	0.543	0.074	0.073	0.315	0.642	0.043	0.828
BE	0.029	0.150	0.121	0.054	0.554	0.071	0.070	0.306	0.647	0.040	0.817
CZ	0.028	0.153	0.124	0.054	0.543	0.075	0.072	0.305	0.656	0.036	0.801
DE	0.033	0.158	0.125	0.054	0.532	0.075	0.080	0.304	0.653	0.046	0.837
ES	0.030	0.157	0.127	0.053	0.537	0.083	0.074	0.329	0.644	0.043	0.841
FR	0.027	0.150	0.122	0.052	0.550	0.072	0.074	0.331	0.644	0.047	0.842
HR	0.035	0.158	0.123	0.054	0.537	0.074	0.071	0.300	0.663	0.039	0.821
IT	0.035	0.155	0.120	0.053	0.542	0.072	0.074	0.295	0.655	0.040	0.836
LU	0.036	0.160	0.124	0.055	0.536	0.075	0.076	0.308	0.643	0.043	0.858
PL	0.033	0.165	0.132	0.055	0.527	0.078	0.073	0.316	0.656	0.036	0.870
PT	0.033	0.161	0.128	0.053	0.530	0.079	0.074	0.324	0.650	0.040	0.854
SK	0.026	0.149	0.123	0.055	0.547	0.076	0.076	0.326	0.658	0.044	0.886

Source: Author's calculations based on BACH (2023).

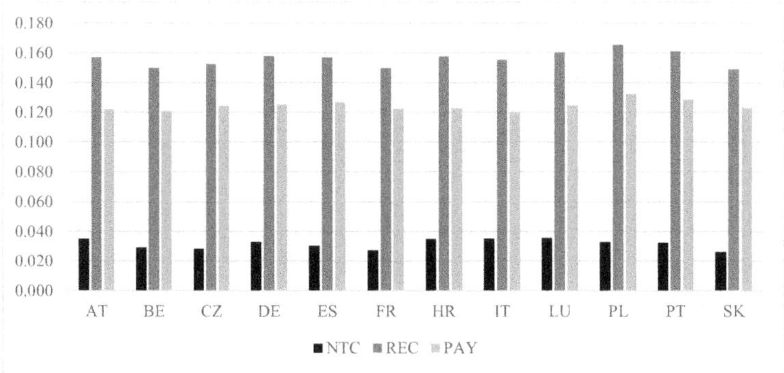

Figure 3.2 Mean values of trade credit ratios across countries.

representation provides insights into the typical levels of these variables and the variations observed among businesses operating in various sectors. It is worth noting that even upon a cursory examination, the variability across industries is considerably more pronounced compared to the variations across size classes or countries.

When examining NTC, notable differences emerge across industries: sectors such as electricity and water supply exhibit higher mean values, while education and administrative activities show negative means, suggesting a deficit. Trade credit granted is highest in manufacturing, mining, quarrying and water supply, indicating that these industries are more inclined to extend credit. In contrast, trade credit obtained is relatively higher in electricity and water supply, reflecting reliance on supplier credit, whereas real estate and professional services exhibit lower dependence.

Analysis of explanatory variables reveals that industries like agriculture, mining and manufacturing show higher values in financing and operational indicators, suggesting greater reliance on short-term bank loans, collateral and inventories. Conversely, sectors such as information and communication, transportation and real estate exhibit lower values, reflecting different financial structures. Profitability and efficiency indicators also vary: arts, entertainment, recreation and education show higher returns on assets and asset turnover, while professional services, information and communication and real estate report lower values. Overall, industry differences in trade credit patterns are

Table 3.3 Mean values of variables across industries

Industry	*Dependent variables*			*Explanatory firm-specific variables*							
	NTC	*REC*	*PAY*	*BKL*	*COL*	*INV*	*CSH*	*CGS*	*DBT*	*ROA*	*TAT*
AGR	0.043	0.167	0.124	0.067	0.548	0.079	0.075	0.323	0.582	0.041	0.846
MIN	0.045	0.177	0.131	0.061	0.535	0.077	0.072	0.312	0.604	0.041	0.856
MNF	0.044	0.185	0.141	0.056	0.521	0.077	0.066	0.293	0.637	0.041	0.924
ELE	0.054	0.199	0.145	0.064	0.499	0.083	0.055	0.292	0.690	0.039	0.844
WAT	0.047	0.180	0.133	0.053	0.512	0.080	0.062	0.281	0.679	0.042	0.799
CST	0.043	0.169	0.127	0.048	0.510	0.080	0.073	0.279	0.675	0.039	0.792
TRD	0.041	0.153	0.111	0.042	0.518	0.075	0.071	0.249	0.699	0.037	0.793
TRS	0.040	0.150	0.110	0.039	0.519	0.067	0.077	0.239	0.690	0.033	0.732
ACF	0.038	0.147	0.109	0.030	0.513	0.069	0.086	0.245	0.687	0.033	0.717
INF	0.022	0.115	0.093	0.040	0.549	0.079	0.083	0.314	0.659	0.037	0.611
REA	0.023	0.084	0.062	0.027	0.553	0.067	0.097	0.310	0.642	0.020	0.611
PRF	0.016	0.084	0.067	0.037	0.578	0.060	0.088	0.336	0.618	0.011	0.667
ADM	-0.002	0.118	0.121	0.047	0.575	0.074	0.082	0.360	0.638	0.039	0.738
EDU	-0.002	0.135	0.137	0.062	0.587	0.069	0.078	0.379	0.653	0.044	0.786
HLT	0.003	0.148	0.145	0.065	0.584	0.071	0.076	0.395	0.659	0.049	0.800
ART	0.005	0.133	0.128	0.056	0.585	0.073	0.083	0.384	0.626	0.065	0.952
OSA	0.026	0.149	0.123	0.055	0.547	0.076	0.076	0.326	0.658	0.044	0.886

Source: Author's calculations based on BACH (2023).

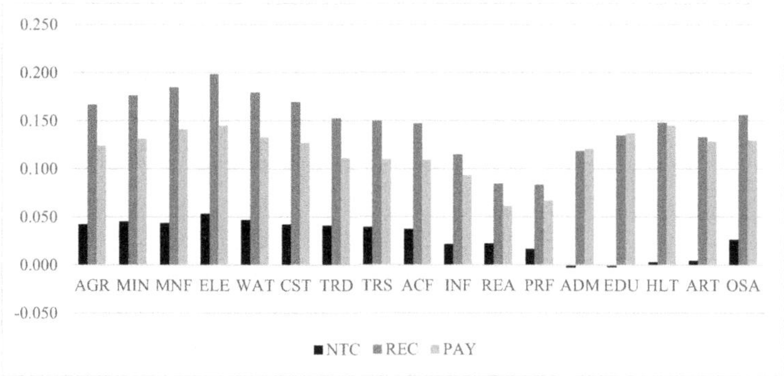

Figure 3.3 Mean values of trade credit ratios across industries.

more pronounced than those across firm size or country, indicating the significant influence of industry-specific factors on financial dynamics.

The issue of variability in parameters that characterise short-term financing of enterprises over time is somewhat situated on the periphery of the primary discourse in this study. Nevertheless, it is worthwhile to consider this aspect in the final stage of basic statistical analysis. Table 3.4 illustrates the average values of the dependent and firm-specific explanatory variables for each consecutive year throughout the analytical period. These average values account for all size categories, countries and industrial sectors included in the study.

Similarly to previously considered cross-sections, the average values of the dependent variables across time are displayed in Figure 3.4. This visual representation provides insights into the typical levels of these variables in each year of the period covering more than two decades.

A brief analysis reveals that NTC exhibits relatively stable mean values over time, indicating a consistent balance between trade credit granted and obtained, with only slight variations. In contrast, trade credit granted and obtained fluctuate more noticeably, showing repeated periods of higher and lower mean values without clear trends, suggesting sensitivity to cyclical economic factors. These two measures generally move in tandem, reflecting a positive correlation between credit extended and received, though the strength of this

Table 3.4 Mean values of variables across time

Year	*Dependent variables*			*Explanatory firm-specific variables*							
	NTC	*REC*	*PAY*	*BKL*	*COL*	*INV*	*CSH*	*CGS*	*DBT*	*ROA*	*TAT*
2000	0.034	0.154	0.120	0.053	0.536	0.076	0.076	0.307	0.649	0.044	0.853
2001	0.033	0.166	0.132	0.056	0.524	0.081	0.073	0.332	0.655	0.041	0.904
2002	0.034	0.155	0.122	0.052	0.542	0.074	0.077	0.294	0.650	0.037	0.780
2003	0.031	0.153	0.121	0.056	0.547	0.073	0.074	0.314	0.651	0.044	0.865
2004	0.030	0.162	0.132	0.055	0.531	0.078	0.073	0.333	0.654	0.042	0.914
2005	0.032	0.154	0.122	0.052	0.548	0.071	0.074	0.294	0.651	0.037	0.783
2006	0.032	0.149	0.117	0.053	0.548	0.073	0.074	0.313	0.642	0.048	0.850
2007	0.030	0.161	0.131	0.055	0.522	0.082	0.073	0.341	0.658	0.038	0.878
2008	0.033	0.153	0.120	0.052	0.550	0.072	0.074	0.298	0.650	0.036	0.767
2009	0.031	0.152	0.120	0.055	0.542	0.074	0.075	0.311	0.651	0.051	0.883
2010	0.031	0.163	0.132	0.055	0.527	0.079	0.074	0.328	0.652	0.052	0.936
2011	0.032	0.153	0.121	0.051	0.549	0.071	0.075	0.289	0.648	0.037	0.784
2012	0.031	0.148	0.118	0.053	0.554	0.070	0.073	0.307	0.648	0.045	0.820
2013	0.031	0.162	0.132	0.055	0.529	0.080	0.073	0.337	0.656	0.041	0.873
2014	0.032	0.153	0.121	0.050	0.549	0.071	0.075	0.294	0.655	0.035	0.757
2015	0.034	0.152	0.117	0.053	0.546	0.075	0.073	0.312	0.649	0.046	0.845
2016	0.030	0.162	0.132	0.056	0.526	0.082	0.072	0.334	0.652	0.039	0.889
2017	0.030	0.152	0.122	0.052	0.551	0.072	0.073	0.298	0.647	0.035	0.773
2018	0.028	0.147	0.119	0.054	0.551	0.073	0.073	0.311	0.643	0.043	0.833
2019	0.033	0.165	0.132	0.056	0.523	0.082	0.074	0.333	0.655	0.043	0.892
2020	0.033	0.155	0.122	0.051	0.546	0.071	0.075	0.296	0.653	0.038	0.777

Source: Author's calculations based on BACH (2023).

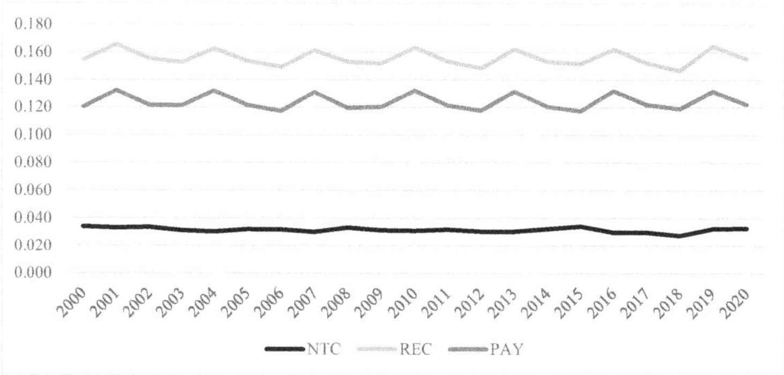

Figure 3.4 Mean values of trade credit ratios across time.

relationship varies over time and may differ when disaggregated by firm size, country, or industry.

Regarding firm-specific explanatory variables, some ratios, such as collateral, cash at hand, debt ratio and total asset turnover, show relative stability over time, suggesting consistent financial practices in asset structure, liquidity management, leverage and asset efficiency. Other ratios, including short-term bank loans, inventory, costs of goods sold and return on assets, display greater variability, indicating shifts in borrowing, inventory management, cost structures and profitability. Overall, the analysis suggests that while some financial indicators remain stable, others reflect evolving financial strategies and performance over the examined period.

To mitigate the potential bias introduced by multicollinearity in the empirical analysis, a correlation analysis was conducted as part of the preliminary investigation into the relationships between variables. The results are presented in Table 3.5, which reports the correlation coefficients for the entire sample, encompassing various size groups, countries, industries and years.

Additionally, Table 3.6 includes values of the variance inflation factor (VIF), a tool utilised to identify multicollinearity in regression analysis.

While numerous significant correlations between variables were identified, the potential multicollinearity issues appear to be minimal. The maximum VIF value for the entire sample is 2.59, which is

Table 3.5 Matrix of correlations for total sample

Ratio	*NTC*	*REC*	*PAY*	*BKL*	*COL*	*INV*	*CSH*	*CGS*	*DBT*	*ROA*
REC	*0.608**									
PAY	0.038*	0.817*								
BKL	0.005	0.233*	0.290*							
COL	-0.408*	-0.769*	-0.670*	-0.202*						
INV	-0.103*	0.276*	0.423*	0.348*	-0.552*					
CSH	0.151*	0.172*	0.107*	-0.105*	-0.387*	-0.049*				
CGS	-0.356*	0.076*	0.354*	0.237*	-0.136*	0.571*	-0.204*			
DBT	0.083*	0.284*	0.298*	0.243*	-0.273*	0.086*	-0.081*	-0.136*		
ROA	0.029*	0.054*	0.047*	-0.021*	-0.106*	-0.030*	0.246*	-0.066*	-0.123*	
TAT	0.037*	0.454*	0.545*	0.121*	-0.468*	0.221*	0.265*	0.258*	0.094*	0.307*

Source: Author's calculations based on BACH (2023).

Note: * – significant at p<0.5.

Table 3.6 Variance inflation factors for total sample

	Dependent variables							
	BKL	*COL*	*INV*	*CSH*	*CGS*	*DBT*	*ROA*	*TAT*
VIF	1,221	2,588	2,576	1,513	1,930	1,308	1,195	1,603

Source: Author's calculations based on BACH (2023).

nearly half the level typically considered to indicate low to moderate multicollinearity, a threshold generally accepted in most cases (Kutner *et al.*, 2005). Correlation values and VIFs were also calculated separately for subsamples defined by firm size, country and industry, although these detailed results are not reported here in full. The findings indicate that multicollinearity among predictor variables within each category of size, country and industry is not a major concern.

3.2 Complementary vs. substitution effect between trade credit and bank loan

In the field of corporate short-term finance research, a fundamental inquiry revolves around the relationship between short-term bank loans and trade credit. At the core of this investigation lies the verification of a crucial research hypothesis, wherein the focus is on discerning the nature of the relationship between these two financing sources. Specifically, the main focus is on determining whether this connection tends to be complementary or substitutionary. In this study, the hypothesis is referred to as **H1**, which states that trade credit and short-term bank loan are complementary, as broadly discussed in Section 2.3. The verification of H1 is based on panel regression results, specifically on the significance and the direction of the relationship between short-term bank loan ratio (BKL) and trade credit measures defined as dependent variables. Significantly positive correlations indicate a complementary effect, wherein both forms of financing augment each other, while significantly negative associations point to a substitution effect, wherein one form of financing tends to supplant the other.

Panel regression results of the equations (2.1.a)–(2.1.c) described in Section 2.4 for total sample are presented in Table 3.7. Following the indications of the Hausman test, the model was estimated as the one that accounts for endogeneity and unobserved heterogeneity (FE)

Table 3.7 Estimation results of panel regression models (2.1.a–c) for total sample

Variable or specification	*Model and dependent variable symbol*					
	(2.1.a) NTC		*(2.1.b) REC*		*(2.1.c) PAY*	
	Estimate	*Std. error*	*Estimate*	*Std. error*	*Estimate*	*Std. error*
const.	0.288^{***}	0.010	0.496^{***}	0.014	0.203^{***}	0.013
BKL	0.109^{***}	0.027	0.127^{***}	0.044		
COL	-0.263^{***}	0.009	-0.540^{***}	0.015	-0.273^{***}	0.013
INV	-0.271^{***}	0.016	-0.403^{***}	0.022	-0.129^{***}	0.019
CSH	-0.209^{***}	0.022	-0.405^{***}	0.027	-0.190^{***}	0.029
CGS	-0.066^{***}	0.005	0.023^{***}	0.008	0.092^{***}	0.007
DBT	-0.066^{***}	0.008	0.018^{*}	0.010	0.088^{***}	0.008
ROA			-0.047^{***}	0.007	-0.036^{***}	0.008
TAT	-0.014^{***}	0.003	0.020^{***}	0.005	0.034^{***}	0.004
SIZE	M^{**}		M^{***}, L^{***}		M^{***}, L^{***}	
CT	none		none		none	
IND	CST^{*}, TRS^{***}, ACF^{***}, INF^{***}, REA^{*}, PRF^{**}, ADM^{***}, EDU^{***}, HLT^{***}, ART^{***}		WAT^{**}, CST^{***}, TRD^{***}, TRS^{***}, ACF^{***}, INF^{***}, REA^{***}, PRF^{***}, ADM^{***}, ART^{**}, OSA^{***}		WAT^{**}, CST^{***}, TRD^{***}, TRS^{***}, ACF^{***}, INF^{***}, REA^{***}, PRF^{***}, EDU^{*}, HLT^{***}, OSA^{***}	

YEAR	2015**	2002*, 2008*, 2014*, 2020*	2002**, 2005**, 2011***, 2014**, 2017**, 2020**
No. obs.	8797	8797	8796
R^2	0.468	0.725	0.663
Adj. R^2	0.467	0.724	0.662
AIC	-30905.0	-27044.9	-29295.1
Hausman test	63.8 [0.000]	249.0 [0.000]	239.7 [0.000]
Wald joint significance robust F test			
SIZE	6.07 [0.014]	17.1 [0.000]	24.1 [0.000]
CT	n/a	n/a	n/a
IND	19.28 [0.000]	12.6 [0.000]	15.3 [0.000]
YEAR	4.43 [0.036]	3.5 [0.008]	5.8 [0.000]

Source: Author's calculations based on (BACH, 2023).

Notes: Interpretation of parameters in relation to small firms for size dummy variables, Austria for country dummy variables and agriculture for industry dummy variables. * – significant at the 10% level, ** – 5%, *** – 1%. For dummy variables values of estimates were replaced with the list of items (symbols of size groups, countries, industries and year numbers) for which the estimate value was significant accompanied by the significance level. Hausman test refers to the pooled OLS model before the inclusion of dummy variables.

with robust errors to address heteroscedasticity and autocorrelation issues.

As previously mentioned, the primary focus of the analysis presented in this section is the coefficient of the explanatory variable termed short-term bank loan denoted as BKL. In models with NTC and trade credit offered (REC) as dependent variables, the coefficient of this variable demonstrates a positive and statistically significant association at conventional significance levels. This indicates a supplementary relationship between these two means of corporate financing. However, for the scenario involving trade credit obtained, the significance of the short-term bank loan ratio is not observed, suggesting the absence of either a complementary or substitution effect between the proportion of accounts payable and short-term bank funding.

The aforementioned observations apply to the entire dataset, spanning various size categories, countries and industries. However, it is also important to analyse the relationship separately within each category. For this purpose, additional estimation models (2.2.a–c), (2.3.a–c) and (2.4.a–c) were carried out individually for different size groups, countries and industries. Table 3.8 offers insights into the validation of research hypotheses (H1a–c) concerning the complementary effect in trade credit. The table's contents provide a synthesised summary of these estimation results, focusing on the significance and direction of the relationship between short-term bank loans and dependent variables in the form of trade credit measures.

Overall, the analysis reveals that the bank loan variable is generally insignificant, indicating the absence of both complementary and substitution effects within the analysed population. This finding holds true for the majority of cases representing approximately 65% of the sample.

However, despite the overall insignificance of the bank loan variable, there is evidence of a prevalent complementary effect. This effect, characterised by a significantly positive relation between short-term bank loans and trade credit, outweighs the substitution effect. It is observed in approximately 24% of the model estimation results, while the substitution effect is found in only 11% of the cases.

These findings lend support to the research hypothesis H1, which suggests the existence of a complementary effect in trade credit. However, further verification is necessary to explore the subhypotheses (a–c) related to different trade credit measures.

Table 3.8 The verification of research hypotheses concerning complementary effect in trade credit (H1a–c)

Sample part		*Hypotheses and trade credit measures*		
		H1a (NTC)	*H1b (REC)*	*H1c (PAY)*
All countries, industries and sizes		complementary	complementary	no effect
Size groups	**SMALL**	complementary	complementary	no effect
	MEDIUM	complementary	substitution	substitution
	LARGE	complementary	no effect	no effect
Countries	**AT**	no effect	complementary	no effect
	BE	no effect	no effect	no effect
	CZ	no effect	no effect	no effect
	DE	no effect	no effect	no effect
	ES	no effect	no effect	no effect
	FR	complementary	no effect	no effect
	HR	no effect	no effect	no effect
	IT	complementary	no effect	no effect
	LU	complementary	complementary	no effect
	PT	no effect	no effect	no effect
	PL	no effect	no effect	no effect
	SK	complementary	complementary	no effect
Industries	**AGR**	complementary	no effect	substitution
	MIN	complementary	no effect	substitution
	MNF	complementary	no effect	no effect
	ELE	complementary	complementary	substitution
	WAT	complementary	no effect	substitution
	CST	complementary	no effect	no effect
	TRD	complementary	no effect	no effect
	TRS	no effect	no effect	no effect
	ACF	no effect	no effect	no effect
	INF	no effect	no effect	no effect
	REA	no effect	complementary	complementary
	PRF	no effect	no effect	no effect
	ADM	no effect	no effect	no effect
	EDU	substitution	substitution	no effect
	HLT	no effect	substitution	substitution
	ART	complementary	no effect	substitution
	OSA	complementary	no effect	no effect

Source: Author's own compilation.

Regarding **H1a**, the hypothesis concerning NTC, there is substantial support for the presence of a complementary effect. In the majority of model estimations (52%), a complementary effect between NTC and other trade credit measures is observed. This effect holds true for the total sample as well as for different size groups. However, the occurrence of the complementary effect weakens when analysing individual countries, as it is only found in four countries.

The finding that a complementary effect in NTC was found in only four countries (FR, IT, LU, SK), while no effect was found in the other countries analysed (AT, BE, CZ, DE, ES, HR, PT, PL) can be explained by several possible factors. One possible explanation is the influence of cultural and business practices. Countries with a stronger tradition of utilising trade credit or a business culture that values trade credit relationships may exhibit a higher likelihood of observing the complementary effect. In contrast, countries where alternative financing options or different payment practices are more prevalent may have a weaker or less pronounced relationship between short-term bank loans and NTC.

Economic factors also play a role. The overall level of economic development, stability and access to financial resources can impact the relationship between short-term bank loans and NTC. Countries with more developed financial markets or greater availability of alternative financing options may experience a diminished complementary effect, as businesses have diverse funding sources beyond trade credit.

The legal and regulatory environment within each country is another important factor. Differences in legal frameworks related to payment terms, credit agreements, or debtor–creditor relationships can influence trade credit practices and the relationship with short-term bank loans. Stricter regulations or standardised payment practices may result in a weaker complementary effect in countries where such regulations are in place.

The composition of industries within each country can also contribute to the variation in findings. Certain industries may have a higher reliance on trade credit, leading to a stronger complementary effect. If the analysed countries have varying industry compositions, it can result in divergent findings regarding the presence of the complementary effect in NTC.

Finally, the size and representation of the sample within each country could also influence the observed results. A relatively small or less representative sample size may introduce biases or limitations that affect the detection of the complementary effect. Additionally, differences in sample characteristics, such as the size or type of businesses included, may contribute to the variation in findings across countries.

Considering these possible factors is crucial for interpreting the results. The combination of cultural, economic, legal and industry-specific elements within each country shapes the prevalence of the complementary effect in NTC.

Moving on to the industrial breakdown of the sample, the detection of the substitution effect exclusively in the education sector, while the complementary effect or no effect prevailed in all other industries analysed, can be attributed to several factors.

First, the nature of the education sector plays a role. Educational institutions have unique financing needs compared to other industries. Factors such as long-term contracts, government funding or specific payment arrangements within the education sector may influence the relationship between short-term bank loans and trade credit, leading to the detection of a substitution effect specific to this industry.

Second, industry-specific financing practices contribute to the observed pattern. In the case of the education sector, the observed substitution effect may reflect the distinctive financial environment in which educational institutions operate. These institutions often rely primarily on public funding, grants and subsidies rather than trade credit or commercial bank loans. Moreover, regulatory frameworks may impose constraints on their financial operations, such as restrictions on borrowing or requirements for balanced budgets, which limit their use of commercial credit arrangements. Additionally, as service-oriented organisations, educational institutions typically have fewer transactions involving inventories or purchases of goods, reducing their need for trade credit.

Furthermore, the dynamics between suppliers and buyers in the education sector may differ from those in other industries. Suppliers in the education sector may have distinct preferences or financial considerations that lead them to offer trade credit differently compared to suppliers in other industries. The nature of the relationships and interactions between suppliers and educational institutions may contribute to the observed substitution effect within the sector.

Moving on to **H1b**, the hypothesis regarding trade credit offered, the support is relatively weak. Only 21% of the model estimation results indicate a complementary effect between trade credit offered and other trade credit measures. While this effect is observed in the total sample, it is predominantly present among small firms, whereas a substitution effect is found among medium-sized firms. When examining individual countries, the occurrence of the complementary effect further diminishes, with only three countries exhibiting it. Regarding the verification of H1b for industries, the findings did not provide support for the hypothesis. Both the complementary and substitution effects were observed in only two industries each, while the majority of sectors exhibited no significant effect.

The likely explanation for finding a substitution effect in trade credit offered for medium firms, a complementary effect for small firms and no effect for large firms can be attributed to various factors related to firm size and financial characteristics. First, medium-sized firms may have specific financing needs and capabilities that differ from small and large firms. These firms often fall in a transitional stage, where they have outgrown the financial constraints of small firms but have not yet reached the scale and resources of large firms. As a result, medium-sized firms may have a greater reliance on short-term bank loans to meet their financing requirements, leading to a substitution effect where they reduce their reliance on trade credit.

On the other hand, small firms typically face more constrained access to external financing, including bank loans. Trade credit becomes a crucial source of working capital for them, allowing them to manage cash flow and maintain relationships with suppliers. As a result, small firms tend to exhibit a complementary effect, where short-term bank loans and trade credit work together to support their financial operations. In contrast, large firms often have greater access to diverse funding options and stronger bargaining power with suppliers. They may have more flexibility in managing their financial resources and can utilise alternative financing methods beyond trade credit. Consequently, the relationship between short-term bank loans and trade credit for large firms tends to show no significant effect.

Additionally, firm-specific characteristics, such as risk profile and financial stability, may also contribute to the observed pattern. Medium-sized firms may be in a position where they need to actively manage their risk exposure and financial leverage. This could lead them to prioritise the substitution of trade credit with short-term bank loans to optimise their financial structure. Small and large firms, with different risk profiles and financial positions, may not exhibit the same level of substitution effect due to varying financial needs and capabilities.

The results concerning complementary versus substitution effect in trade credit offered across industries suggest that the relationship between short-term bank loans and accounts receivable in most industries is not influenced by either the complementary or substitution effect. In these sectors, other factors or financing mechanisms likely play a more prominent role in shaping firms' decisions regarding trade credit and bank loans. The limited occurrence of the complementary and substitution effects in specific industries highlights the industry-specific factors influencing these patterns. Certain industries may have unique characteristics or financing practices that make them more conducive to the emergence of these effects. However, in the majority of sectors, the absence of significant effects suggests that factors other than short-term bank loans are the primary drivers of trade credit decisions.

In contrast to H1b and particularly to H1a, the hypothesis **H1c**, concerning trade credit received, finds minimal support. The complementary effect is identified in only one model estimation for the real estate industry, while the substitution effect is observed for large firms and six industries. Short-term bank loans generally prove insignificant across all countries and most industries, providing no support for H1c.

The varying levels of support for H1a, H1b and H1c displayed in Table 3.8 can be explained by several factors. First, the nature of the trade credit measures themselves plays a role. H1a, which examines NTC, considers the overall trade credit position, combining both trade credit offered and trade credit received. This comprehensive view may lead to a more evident complementary effect, explaining the support it receives in the analysis.

On the other hand, H1b focuses specifically on trade credit offered. The decision-making process regarding trade credit offered by businesses may be influenced by factors beyond the scope of trade credit received. As a result, the support for the complementary effect in H1b is weaker compared to H1a, indicating that trade credit offered may not consistently align with the presence of short-term bank loans.

In the case of H1c, which examines trade credit received, the rejection of the hypothesis suggests that the availability or inclination of suppliers to provide trade credit may not be strongly influenced by the presence of short-term bank loans. Factors such as supplier preferences, market conditions or alternative financing options could influence the absence of a complementary effect in trade credit received.

Another factor contributing to the varying levels of support is the variation across different sample characteristics. The analysis reveals that H1a receives support across different size groups, indicating that the complementary effect in NTC is consistent regardless of company size. However, the weaker support for H1b suggests that the influence of trade credit offered on short-term bank loans may vary based on firm size. Similarly, the absence of support for H1c in most countries and industries suggests that the relationship between trade credit received and short-term bank loans may be influenced by specific contextual factors.

To summarise, the findings highlight the prevalence of the complementary effect in NTC (H1a), while support for the complementary effect in trade credit offered (H1b) is relatively weak. The hypothesis regarding trade credit received (H1c) receives no support, as the complementary effect is limited in its occurrence.

3.3 Corporate short-term finance across size groups of firms

As discussed in the preceding sub-chapter, the results of panel regression for individual size groups are presented. These estimation outcomes serve as the foundation for validating hypotheses (H2a–c), which focus on the significance of the industry effect in trade credit as compared to the country effect. The relative importance of these two effects was assessed based on the significance of the corresponding dummy variables for both countries and industries. Table 3.9 offers

Table 3.9 The verification of research hypotheses concerning the relative importance of industry versus country effect in trade credit (H2a–c)

Sample part		*Hypotheses and trade credit measures*		
		H2a (NTC)	*H2b (REC)*	*H2c (PAY)*
All countries, industries and sizes		industry	industry	industry
Size groups	**SMALL**	industry	industry, country	industry, country
	MEDIUM	industry, country	industry, country	industry, country
	LARGE	industry	industry	industry

Source: Author's own compilation.

Note: The table indicates significant effects for each sub-hypothesis and sample part.

insights into the validation of research hypotheses (H2a–c) through a synthesised summary that enumerates the significant effects.

The findings from Table 3.9 reveal support for the predominance of the industry effect over the country effect in trade credit across the total sample and for all three trade credit measures. However, the results become more ambiguous when examining the verification of H2 separately for each size category of firms.

Specifically, H2a, which pertains to NTC, is supported for both small and large firms. However, for medium-sized firms, both the industry effect and the country effect were found to be significant, indicating a more complex relationship.

Regarding H2b and H2, they were strongly supported only for large firms, suggesting that the industry effect prevails over the country effect in terms of trade credit offered and obtained. In contrast, for small and medium firms, both effects were found to be significant for both trade credit offered and obtained, indicating that neither effect can be exclusively considered as more influential. This lack of exclusive significance for H2b and H2c in the case of small and medium firms suggests that these hypotheses are not supported for these two size classes.

In summary, the analysis indicates that H2a, H2b and H2c are supported for the total sample and for large firms. Additionally, H2a is supported for small firms. These findings suggest that the relative importance of the industry effect increases with firm size in the context of trade credit received and offered. Otherwise, the results indicate a diminishing role of country-specific features for large companies in terms of trade credit. This suggests that the influence of country-level factors becomes less significant compared to the industry-specific factors when it comes to trade credit policies for larger firms.

The decreasing role of country-specific features for large companies in terms of trade credit can be attributed to several factors. First, the increasing globalisation and internationalisation of businesses have expanded the reach of large companies beyond national boundaries. As some of them engage in cross-border trade, their trade credit decisions become influenced more by industry-specific factors that transcend individual countries. The focus shifts towards considering global market dynamics rather than country-specific features.

Second, the standardisation of trade practices across countries has contributed to the diminishing significance of country-specific features. With the alignment of trade standards and practices, large companies adopt standardised trade credit policies that are consistent across their global operations. This standardisation minimises the impact of specific country factors on trade credit decisions.

The scale economies enjoyed by larger firms play a part in the increasing significance of the industry effect. As firms grow in size, they can benefit from economies of scale. This advantage allows them to leverage their size and volume of transactions to negotiate more favourable trade credit terms within their industry. As a result, the industry effect becomes stronger in trade credit as firm size increases.

Moreover, the risk diversification strategies employed by large companies play a role in reducing the influence of country-specific features. These companies have greater resources and capabilities to manage risks associated with cross-border trade. They utilise sophisticated risk management techniques and have access to a wider range of financial instruments, allowing them to mitigate country-specific risks. Consequently, their trade credit decisions become less reliant on country-specific factors.

Industry-specific dynamics might also contribute to the diminishing role of country-specific features. As companies grow larger, they often become more specialised within their industries, developing deep expertise and relationships within those sectors. This specialisation leads to industry-specific factors playing a more prominent role in trade credit decisions, overshadowing the influence of country-specific features.

Additionally, the access to resources and information available to larger firms contributes to the increasing importance of the industry effect. Larger firms typically have more abundant resources, including financial stability and extensive information networks. These resources allow them to gather industry-specific information, assess risks effectively and make informed decisions regarding trade credit. Consequently, their access to resources intensifies the industry effect in trade credit.

Lastly, the negotiating power of large companies is an important factor in diminishing the role of country-specific features. Due to their size and market dominance, these companies often have stronger bargaining positions with suppliers regardless of their location. This increased negotiating power empowers them to have more control over trade credit terms, reducing the significance of country-specific factors in the decision-making process.

Taken together, these factors contribute to the diminishing importance of country-specific features for large companies in the area of trade credit. The global nature of their operations, standardisation of trade practices, risk management strategies, industry dynamics and negotiating power all shift the focus towards industry-specific considerations rather than country-specific features in their trade credit policies.

When considering the cross-size section in terms of corporate short-term financing decisions, it is also relevant to identify and compare the impact of explanatory variables on trade credit and therefore verify the research hypothesis **H5**, which states that the significance and direction of the impact of explanatory variables on trade credit differs across size groups of firms. Table 3.10 provides calculation results of the similarity index for the relationships between explanatory and dependent variables across size groups. The higher the values, the more similar the impact of a given factor on trade credit measure.

Table 3.10 Cross-size similarity index of the relationship between explanatory and dependent variables

Explanatory variable	*Dependent variable*			*Average*
	NTC	*REC*	*PAY*	
BKL	1.00	0.00	0.33	**0.44**
COL	1.00	1.00	1.00	**1.00**
INV	1.00	1.00	0.33	**0.78**
CSH	1.00	1.00	1.00	**1.00**
CGS	1.00	0.00	1.00	**0.67**
DBT	1.00	0.00	1.00	**0.67**
ROA	1.00	0.33	0.33	**0.55**
TAT	1.00	1.00	1.00	**1.00**
CT	0.33	0.33	0.33	**0.33**
IND	1.00	1.00	1.00	**1.00**
YEAR	0.33	0.33	0.33	**0.33**
Average	**0.88**	**0.54**	**0.70**	**0.71**

Source: Author's calculations.

Notes: The values represent the percentage share of cases for which the impact on trade credit was similar between size groups through pairwise comparisons. Similarity indicates either significantly positive relation in two size classes compared, significantly negative relation in both groups, or insignificant in both groups. In the case of dummy variables, similarity indicates that the joint impact of a given category of variables (country, industry or year dummy variables) was either significant or insignificant for the two compared size classes.

In analysing the impact of firm-related variables on NTC, the findings reveal a similar impact across all size classes, suggesting the rejection of hypothesis H5a. However, when considering the other two trade credit measures, the impact of firm-related variables appears more varied. Specifically, in the case of trade credit granted, three variables exhibit different relationships in each size class, as reflected by the 0% similarity indexes. This provides strong support for hypothesis H5b.

Regarding trade credit received, the impact shows less variation, with only three variables demonstrating different relationships with accounts payable ratio in one size class. This provides weaker support for hypothesis H5c.

Several variables can be classified as stable, meaning their impact on trade credit remains similar regardless of the size class. These variables include collateral, cash, total assets turnover and industry dummy variables. Conversely, there are variables whose impact on trade credit varies across size groups, including short-term bank loan, return on assets, costs of goods sold and debt ratio. Industry dummy variables consistently exhibit significance across size classes, while the importance of country and year dummy variables differs depending on the size class.

In summary, hypothesis H5a is rejected, hypothesis H5b is supported and hypothesis H5c is weakly supported. This provides further support for the occurrence of the indirect size effect in trade credit. If the direct effect is understood as the significance of size dummy variables included in the models explaining trade credit measures, then the indirect effect might be demonstrated in the cross-size variation of direct trade credit factors' impact on it. Therefore, it can be stated that while no indirect size effect is observed in the case of NTC, this secondary influence of size becomes noticeable when examining trade credit obtained and is even more pronounced for trade credit offered. Several factors may contribute to this disparity.

First, the dynamics of supplier–buyer relationships could play a role. Larger suppliers may have greater bargaining power and extend favourable credit terms to smaller buyers, resulting in a stronger impact of supplier size on credit obtained. Conversely, the size of the buyer may influence the credit terms offered, as larger buyers are often perceived as more financially stable and trustworthy by suppliers.

Second, risk perception could contribute to the observed differences. Smaller businesses seeking trade credit may face higher risk assessments from suppliers, leading to stricter credit terms. In contrast, larger businesses offering trade credit may be viewed as more reliable, allowing them to offer more lenient credit terms to smaller buyers.

Additionally, financial capacity may influence this relationship, with larger businesses having greater resources to provide more attractive credit terms. Smaller businesses, constrained by financial limitations, may be subject to more stringent credit terms.

Finally, market competition can influence the indirect size effect. In highly competitive markets, businesses may offer more favourable credit terms to attract customers and gain a competitive edge, thereby intensifying the influence of size on trade credit offered.

These factors might jointly contribute to the observed pattern where the indirect size effect is absent in NTC but becomes pronounced when examining trade credit obtained and offered.

3.4 Corporate short-term finance across countries

The results of panel regressions were also obtained separately for distinct countries. These estimation results constitute the groundwork for validating hypotheses (H3a-c) regarding the importance of the industry impact on trade credit compared to the size impact. The relative importance of these two influences was evaluated by examining the significance of the corresponding dummy variables for industries and size categories. Table 3.11 provides insights into the substantiation of research hypotheses (H3a–c) via a condensed summary that lists the significant effects.

The synthetic summary of the findings reported in Table 3.11 indicates that when considering the entire sample, both the size and industry effects are significant for all three trade credit measures (NTC, REC and PAY). This suggests that there is no support for H3, at least for the total population examined. However, a more detailed view emerges when examining individual countries along with the three trade credit measures separately.

Regarding NTC (H3a), the industry effect clearly prevails in most countries, with the size effect being insignificant. Exceptions to this trend are observed in Austria and Germany, where both effects are significant, and in Italy, where neither effect proves significant.

When considering trade credit granted (H3b), the relative importance of the industry effect compared to the size effect weakens. Only

Table 3.11 The verification of research hypotheses concerning the relative importance of industry versus size effect in trade credit (H3a–c)

Sample part		*Hypotheses and trade credit measures*		
		H3a (NTC)	*H3b (REC)*	*H3c (PAY)*
All countries, industries and sizes		size, industry	size, industry	size, industry
Countries	**AT**	size, industry	size, industry	size, industry
	BE	industry	size, industry	size, industry
	CZ	industry	size, industry	size, industry
	DE	size, industry	industry	size, industry
	ES	industry	size, industry	size, industry
	FR	industry	size, industry	size, industry
	HR	industry	size, industry	size, industry
	IT	none	industry	size, industry
	LU	industry	size, industry	industry
	PT	industry	size, industry	size, industry
	PL	industry	industry	size, industry
	SK	industry	industry	industry

Source: Author's own compilation.

Note: The table indicates significant effects for each sub-hypothesis and sample part.

four countries (Germany, Italy, Poland and Slovakia) demonstrate the significance of the industry effect accompanied by the insignificance of size-related features.

The impact of the industry effect becomes even less pronounced when examining trade credit obtained (H3c), with the clear prevalence of the industry effect over the size effect reported in only two countries (Luxembourg and Slovakia). In the remaining countries, where both effects are meaningful, the dominant effect was not determined.

In general, for most individual countries, both the size and industry effects prove meaningful when estimating the models. No cases were found where the size effect prevailed over the industry effect.

In summary, there is support found for H3a in most countries, while H3b and H3c receive weaker support. However, based on the results, there are no grounds to reject H3.

Several likely explanations account for the industry effect being stronger than the size effect for NTC. First, industries often develop their own unique practices and norms regarding trade credit, which heavily influence the level of NTC extended by firms. These industry-specific practices can minimise the influence of firm size on NTC decisions.

Second, as in the case of comparing the industry and country effect, the relative power dynamics between suppliers and buyers might be a contributing factor. In some industries, suppliers may have greater bargaining power, allowing them to offer more favourable credit terms. Intense competition within certain industries can also drive firms to use NTC strategically to gain a competitive edge. These industry-specific supplier power dynamics and market competition contribute to a stronger industry effect on NTC.

Additionally, different industries exhibit varying levels of financial risks, such as default risk or insolvency risk. These industry-specific risks can affect firms' NTC decisions. Industries with higher perceived risk levels may tighten their credit policies, resulting in lower NTC. The industry effect on NTC is thus strengthened by industry-specific risk considerations.

Moreover, industries can differ in the financial stability and creditworthiness of their customers. Industries with customers who have better financial positions and credit ratings may extend higher levels of NTC. Conversely, industries with customers facing financial challenges may restrict NTC to mitigate credit risk. This variation in the financial stability and creditworthiness of customers contributes to the industry effect on NTC.

Lastly, certain industries are more susceptible to economic factors, such as economic cycles, market demand fluctuations or industry-specific trends. Industries experiencing economic downturns, for example, may tighten credit terms to minimise financial risks.

In summary, the industry effect being stronger than the size effect for NTC is likely due to industry-specific practices, supplier power dynamics, industry-specific risks, the financial stability and creditworthiness of customers and industry-specific economic factors. The collection of these factors may contribute to the dominance of the industry effect in influencing NTC decisions.

When examining corporate short-term financing decisions in the international cross-section, it becomes relevant to explore and compare how explanatory variables impact trade credit in individual countries. This exploration aims to validate hypothesis **H6**, which proposes that the significance and direction of these explanatory variables' impact on trade credit vary among countries. The findings, presented in Table 3.12, include a similarity index that measures the resemblance

Table 3.12 Cross-country similarity index of the relationship between explanatory and dependent variables

Explanatory variable	*Dependent variable*			*Average*
	NTC	*REC*	*PAY*	
BKL	0.52	0.59	1.00	**0.70**
COL	1.00	1.00	1.00	**1.00**
INV	1.00	1.00	0.70	**0.90**
CSH	1.00	1.00	0.59	**0.86**
CGS	1.00	0.70	0.70	**0.80**
DBT	1.00	0.70	0.83	**0.84**
ROA	0.83	0.47	0.45	**0.59**
TAT	0.59	0.52	0.59	**0.57**
SIZE	0.70	0.52	0.68	**0.63**
IND	0.83	1.00	1.00	**0.94**
YEAR	0.83	1.00	1.00	**0.94**
Average	**0.85**	**0.77**	**0.78**	**0.80**

Source: Author's calculations.

Notes: The values represent the percentage share of cases for which the impact on trade credit was similar between countries through pairwise comparisons. Similarity indicates either significantly positive relation in two countries compared, significantly negative relation in both countries, or insignificant in both countries. In the case of dummy variables, similarity indicates that the joint impact of a given category of variables (country, industry or year dummy variables) was either significant or insignificant for the two compared countries.

of relationships between explanatory and dependent variables in the international cross-section. Similar to the cross-size section discussed earlier, higher values of this index indicate a more comparable impact of a particular factor on the trade credit measure.

Upon examining the results, it is evident that most firm-related variables exhibit a similar impact on net trade credit, indicating very weak support for hypothesis H6a. However, when considering the other trade credit measures, i.e., trade credit offered and granted, the impact of firm-related variables appears to be somewhat more diverse, providing some support for hypotheses H6b and H6c.

Among the variables analysed, collateral stands out as the most stable one, with a consistent impact on trade credit regardless of the country. On the other hand, variables such as total assets turnover, ROA and size dummy variables display significant variations in their impact on trade credit across countries.

The impact of industry and year dummy variables is equally important for both trade credit offered and received, indicating their comparable relevance across countries. However, the significance of size dummy variables varies across countries for all trade credit measures, highlighting the differences in their effect depending on the specific country context.

In summary, the findings suggest no support for hypothesis H6a, while weak yet noticeable support can be inferred for hypotheses H6b and H6c.

Overall, the aforementioned findings offer limited support for the existence of an indirect country effect on trade credit. This effect refers to the cross-country variation in the relationship between trade credit and its underlying factors, as opposed to the direct impact of specific countries, which is assessed by including country dummy variables in the estimations.

The observed weak indirect country effect in trade credit can be attributed to several factors. First, if the industry under analysis is relatively homogeneous across countries, it may minimise the cross-country variability in the relationship between trade credit and its determinants. When businesses in different countries adopt similar practices and policies, regardless of their location, it reduces the impact of country-specific factors on trade credit. Moreover, the increased globalisation and standardisation of business practices across countries contribute to a convergence in trade credit policies. As firms gain access to international financial markets and alternative sources of financing, their reliance on trade credit as a means of financing decreases, weakening the indirect country effect. Additionally, trade agreements and harmonisation efforts among countries can lead to the alignment of trade credit practices and regulations, reducing the cross-country variation. Finally, institutional factors, such as variations in legal systems, contract enforcement and institutional frameworks, can influence trade credit practices. However, if these institutional differences are limited or if businesses adapt their practices to mitigate these differences, the indirect country effect on trade credit may be weakened. Overall, these factors explain the limited support for the indirect country effect observed in trade credit.

3.5 Corporate short-term finance across industries

Similar to previous sub-chapters, panel regressions were also estimated separately for individual industrial sections. These estimation outcomes serve as the basis for validating hypotheses (H4a–c), which focus on the significance of the country effect in trade credit as compared to the firm size effect. The relative importance of these two effects was evaluated based on the significance of the corresponding dummy variables for countries and size classes. Table 3.13 displays information regarding the examination of research hypotheses (H4a–c) through a synthesised summary that lists the significant effects.

For the entire sample, the results regarding H4 indicate support for the hypotheses. The size effect was found to be significant for all three trade credit measures, while the country effect was found to be insignificant. This suggests that size-related factors play a more prominent role compared to country-related factors in determining trade credit levels.

Table 3.13 The verification of research hypotheses concerning the relative importance of size versus country effect in trade credit (H4a–c)

Sample part		*Hypotheses and trade credit measures*		
		H4a (NTC)	*H4b (REC)*	*H4c (PAY)*
All countries, industries and sizes		size	size	size
Industries	**AGR**	size, country	size, country	size
	MIN	size, country	size, country	size, country
	MNF	country	size, country	size
	ELE	size, country	size, country	size, country
	WAT	country	size, country	size
	CST	country	size, country	size, country
	TRD	size, country	country	size, country
	TRS	country	size, country	size, country
	ACF	country	country	country
	INF	size, country	country	size, country
	REA	country	size, country	size, country
	PRF	size, country	size, country	size, country
	ADM	country	size, country	size
	EDU	size, country	size, country	size, country
	HLT	size	size, country	size, country
	ART	country	size, country	size, country
	OSA	size, country	size, country	size

Source: Author's own compilation.

Note: The table indicates significant effects for each sub-hypothesis and sample part.

However, when examining the relative importance of the two effects across different industries and trade credit measures, variations become apparent. For **H4a**, which focuses on NTC, the significance of only the size effect was found in the healthcare sector. In eight industries, country-related factors were more important than size-related factors, leading to the rejection of H4a. In cases where both effects were found to be significant, it was not determined which effect held more importance.

In the case of **H4b**, which explores REC, the country effect was found to be more important in three industrial sectors. In other industries, both effects were significant, thereby failing to provide support for H4b.

Conversely, for **H4c**, which investigates trade credit received, the size effect was found to be more important than country-related features in five industries. This finding provides weak support for H3c. Only the accommodation sector exhibited a higher influence of country-related factors over size-related ones, while in most sectors (11), both effects were found to be relevant.

The differences in the prominence of the country effect compared to the size effect for NTC, trade credit offered and trade credit received can be attributed to various factors. First, market entry barriers may play a significant role. Certain industries or markets may have higher barriers to entry, particularly in foreign markets. In such cases, country-related factors such as legal frameworks, regulatory compliance, cultural differences and market knowledge become more influential. This can overshadow the impact of company size and financial strength on NTC and trade credit offered.

Second, the power dynamics between suppliers and buyers in international trade can contribute to the observed differences. Suppliers from specific countries might possess a stronger bargaining position or established trade networks. As a result, the country effect becomes more pronounced for NTC and trade credit offered. Suppliers rely on country-related factors to negotiate trade credit terms, while the size effect may have a relatively smaller impact.

Furthermore, risk perception and mitigation play a role in shaping the prominence of the country effect. Companies offering trade credit are often concerned about the risks associated with non-payment or delayed payment. If certain countries are perceived to carry higher risks in terms of economic stability, political conditions, legal frameworks or payment behaviours, the country effect becomes more influential.

Suppliers prioritise country-related factors to mitigate potential risks, overshadowing the influence of buyer size.

On the other hand, for trade credit received, the size effect becomes more pronounced due to buyer-specific factors. Companies receiving trade credit are typically evaluated based on their own financial strength, creditworthiness and ability to repay. Suppliers providing trade credit consider buyer size as an indicator of creditworthiness and the ability to fulfil payment obligations. In this context, the country effect may have a relatively lesser impact as it becomes secondary to the buyer's financial stability.

Lastly, industry-specific practices contribute to the observed differences. Different industries may have specific norms and practices regarding trade credit. In some industries, buyer size is considered a critical factor in determining trade credit received, as larger companies are often associated with higher creditworthiness and greater financial resources. Conversely, other industries may place more emphasis on country-related factors due to specific industry characteristics or supplier–buyer relationships.

In summary, H4a and H4b were rejected based on the findings, indicating that the relative importance of size and country effects varies across industries and trade credit measures. H4c received weak support, as the size effect proved to be more significant than country-related features in several sectors.

Similar to previously discussed cross-sections, when analysing corporate short-term financing decisions across different industries, it becomes essential to examine and compare how explanatory variables influence trade credit. This analysis aims to validate research hypothesis **H7**, which posits that the significance and direction of the impact of explanatory variables on trade credit vary depending on the industrial sectors. Table 3.14 presents the calculated results of a similarity index, which measures the similarity between relationships involving explanatory and dependent variables across industries. Larger values of the index indicate a greater resemblance in the impact of a particular determinant on the trade credit measure across different industrial sectors.

Upon analysing the data, it is apparent that most firm-related variables exhibit a quite varied impact on trade credit, indicating substantial support for hypothesis H7. This variability is observed across the three trade credit measures, suggesting consistent support for all three sub-hypotheses H7a, H7b and H7c.

Table 3.14 Cross-industry similarity index of the relationship between explanatory and dependent variables

Explanatory variable	*Dependent variable*			*Average*
	NTC	*REC*	*PAY*	
BKL	0.42	0.59	0.38	**0.46**
COL	0.88	1.00	0.78	**0.89**
INV	0.60	0.53	0.60	**0.58**
CSH	0.56	0.69	0.68	**0.64**
CGS	0.78	0.31	0.49	**0.53**
DBT	0.62	0.45	0.48	**0.52**
ROA	0.48	0.41	0.51	**0.47**
TAT	0.48	0.51	0.88	**0.62**
SIZE	0.46	0.69	0.88	**0.68**
CT	0.88	1.00	0.56	**0.81**
YEAR	0.62	0.51	0.69	**0.61**
Average	**0.62**	**0.61**	**0.63**	**0.62**

Source: Author's calculations.

Notes: The values represent the percentage share of cases for which the impact on trade credit was similar between industries through pairwise comparisons. Similarity indicates either significantly positive relation in a pair of industries being compared, significantly negative relation in both industries, or insignificant in both industries. In the case of dummy variables, similarity indicates that the joint impact of a given category of variables (country, industry or year dummy variables) was either significant or insignificant for the pair of sectors under comparison.

Regarding stable variables, collateral stands out as the only one whose impact on trade credit is similar regardless of the industry, but only for trade credit offered. On the contrary, the variables with the most significant variations in their impact on trade credit across industries are return on assets (ROA) and bank loan ratio.

Furthermore, the importance of size, country and year dummy variables also differs across industries for all trade credit measures, with the exception of country dummy variables for trade credit offered, where their importance remains consistent across all industries.

In summary, the findings demonstrate the substantial and diverse impact of firm-specific and dummy variables across industries, providing robust support for hypothesis H7 and its three sub-hypotheses. This analysis reveals the significance of considering the industrial sector's context when studying corporate short-term financing decisions.

References

BACH (2023) *Bank for the Accounts of Companies Harmonized*. Banque de France, www.bach.banque-france.fr

Kutner, M.H. *et al.* (2005) *Applied Linear Statistical Models*. Fifth. Boston: McGraw-Hill Irwin.

4 Conclusions

At its conceptual core, the study offers a detailed and critical theoretical framework for understanding short-term corporate financing, describing the full spectrum of instruments available to firms – including trade credit, short-term bank loans, factoring, commercial paper and emerging alternatives such as private credit and fintech-driven liquidity solutions. These instruments are examined not only in terms of their structural characteristics but also their strategic roles in managing operational risk, sustaining working capital and addressing financial constraints.

The analysis demonstrates that short-term finance occupies a key position in firms' financial structure, particularly in contexts marked by heightened volatility, institutional limitations or restricted access to long-term capital markets. Trade credit is shown to function as both a financial and relational tool – supporting deferred payment while simultaneously strengthening supply chain stability and commercial trust. In contrast, bank loans are framed as more formalised and institutionally mediated instruments, dependent on firms' credit profiles, collateral availability and banking relationships.

The theoretical discussion is grounded in several foundational models, including transaction cost economics, the financing advantage hypothesis and price discrimination theory, each of which is used to interpret firms' financing choices within the structurally diverse European financial environment. Building on this foundation, the study offers a critical evaluation of the theoretical debate surrounding the substitutive and complementary roles of trade credit and short-term bank loans. The literature review reveals that these two financing instruments are not inherently exclusive but rather serve overlapping functions depending

DOI: 10.4324/9781003687986-4

on firms' access to institutional credit, risk exposure and strategic priorities. According to the substitution hypothesis, trade credit acts as a second-best alternative when bank loans are limited or unavailable, particularly for financially constrained or smaller firms. The complementarity hypothesis suggests that both forms of finance can co-exist and support one another, especially within firms that maintain stable credit relationships and seek to optimise liquidity across multiple channels. The discussion highlights that the relationship is contingent, dynamic and often cyclical – shaped by firm-level characteristics, industry structure and broader economic fluctuations – emphasising the need for context-sensitive interpretations of short-term financing behaviour.

Extending the theoretical insights, the study presents a comprehensive review of the determinants influencing corporate short-term financing decisions. These determinants are categorised into firm-specific, industry-specific and country-level factors, each contributing differently to the configuration of trade credit and bank loan usage. The analysis systematically examines how variables such as collateral availability, liquidity, profitability, leverage and operational efficiency shape firms' ability to obtain and extend short-term credit. Firm size emerges as a particularly significant factor, with smaller enterprises generally more reliant on trade credit due to their limited access to institutional finance, while larger firms exhibit more diversified financing structures. Industry effects are also pronounced, especially in capital-intensive sectors or those with long operating cycles, where specific financing patterns reflect sectoral norms and working capital dynamics.

The discussion further incorporates the macro-institutional context, demonstrating that national legal frameworks, banking sector development, cultural norms and regulatory environments can substantially affect the availability and use of short-term financing instruments. Remarkably, the country effect is particularly pronounced among micro and small enterprises, which are more exposed to local financial infrastructures and institutional constraints. The analysis also highlights the sensitivity of short-term financing behaviour to external shocks, with financial crises and global disruptions such as the COVID-19 pandemic intensifying firms' reliance on trade credit when access to bank loans becomes constrained.

Theoretical insights into the complex and interrelated factors influencing short-term financing decisions provide a coherent framework for analysis, laying the groundwork for the empirical investigation and leading to a more detailed interpretation of the observed patterns in corporate financing behaviour.

The empirical analysis was designed in alignment with the research aims of the study. Specifically, it aimed to assess whether trade credit and short-term bank loans function as complementary or substitutable sources of corporate short-term financing and to evaluate the relative importance of country, industry and firm size in shaping firms' short-term financing decisions. These objectives were pursued through a structured examination of harmonised financial data, with the analysis applied not only to the aggregated sample but also disaggregated by firm size, national context and sectoral affiliation. This approach allowed for a detailed exploration of financing patterns across diverse corporate environments, reflecting the multidimensional nature of short-term financial behaviour.

Table 4.1 presents a concise overview of the research hypotheses' verification (H1–H7). The table is structured to show the abbreviated formulation of hypotheses, the corresponding sample parts or cross-sections where they were tested and the sub-hypothesis index for

Table 4.1 The summary of research hypotheses' verification (H1–H7)

Hypothesis	*Sample part or cross-section*	*Sub-hypothesis index and trade credit measures*		
		a (NTC)	*b (REC)*	*c (PAY)*
H1 (complementary effect > substitution effect)	Total	++	++	0
	Size groups	++	0	–
	Countries	+	+	0
	Industries	++	0	–
H2 (industry effect > country effect)	Total	++	++	++
	Size groups	++	+	+
H3 (industry effect > size effect)	Total	0	0	0
	Countries	++	+	+
H4 (size effect > country effect)	Total	++	++	++
	Industries	–	–	+
H5 (different impact of variables across size groups)	Cross-size comparisons	–	++	+
H6 (different impact of variables across countries)	Cross-country comparisons	0	+	+
H7 (different impact of variables across industries)	Cross-industry comparisons	++	++	++

Source: Author's own compilation.

Notes: "++" indicates strong support. "+" – weak support. "0" – no support and "–" indicates rejection.

each trade credit measure (NTC – net trade credit, REC – trade credit granted, PAY – trade credit obtained). The results show strong support for certain hypotheses in the total sample, but weaker support or rejection in specific subgroups, indicating complexities in analysing factors influencing corporate short-term financing decisions across different contexts.

H1, which examines the complementary effect compared to the substitution effect, was tested across different sample parts. In the total sample, there is strong support, indicating that the complementary effect outweighs the substitution effect for two out of three trade credit measures. However, when considering size groups and in countries, the support is somewhat weaker. For size groups, strong support is found in NTC and weak support in trade credit granted (REC), while for countries, there is moderate support in both NTC and trade credit granted but no support in trade credit obtained (PAY.

H2, focusing on the industry effect compared to the country effect, was verified in the total sample and size groups. The results show strong support for H2 in total sample, indicating that the industry effect has a more significant impact on all three trade credit measures compared to the country effect. Similar patterns are observed when considering size groups, with strong support in NTC and weak support in trade credit granted.

H3, examining the industry effect compared to the size effect, was tested in the total sample and countries. For the total sample, there is no support across all trade credit measures, suggesting that the industry effect and size effect have comparable impacts. However, for countries, there is strong support in NTC and weak support in trade credit granted, indicating that the industry effect has a more substantial impact on trade credit compared to the size effect in these cases.

H4, which investigates the size effect compared to the country effect, was verified in the total sample and industries. In the total sample, there is strong support, indicating that the size effect has a more significant impact on all three trade credit measures compared to the country effect. However, for industries, there is rejection in both NTC and trade credit granted, meaning that the size effect is less influential than the country effect for these trade credit measures.

H5 examines the different impacts of variables across size groups through cross-size comparisons. The results show rejection in NTC, strong support in trade credit granted and weak support in trade credit obtained, indicating varying impacts of variables across different size groups for these trade credit measures.

H6 investigates the different impacts of variables across countries through cross-country comparisons. For NTC, there is no support, implying that the impact of variables is consistent across countries. However, for trade credit granted, there is weak support, indicating some variations in the impact of variables across countries. In trade credit obtained, there is strong support, indicating a more pronounced difference in the impact of variables across countries.

H7 focuses on the different impact of variables across industries through cross-industry comparisons. The results show strong support for all trade credit measures, suggesting significant variations in the impact of variables across different industrial sectors.

In summary, Table 4.1 provides an overview of the research hypotheses' verification. The varying levels of support or rejection indicate the complexities involved in analysing the factors influencing corporate short-term financing decisions across different sample parts and cross-sections.

The findings of this study also open several paths for future research. First, further investigation is needed into how digital financial technologies and non-bank financing platforms are reshaping short-term financing strategies, particularly for SMEs. Second, while this study focuses on established EU economies, comparative research including emerging European markets or non-EU countries could yield additional insights into institutional influences. Third, a longitudinal perspective examining post-crisis behavioural shifts – especially in response to recent regulatory changes or ESG-driven financing priorities – would enrich the understanding of firms' evolving liquidity management. Finally, qualitative approaches, including case studies or interviews, could complement quantitative analyses by capturing managerial rationales behind short-term financing decisions in different organisational and national contexts.

Taken together, the theoretical and empirical findings of the study offer a detailed and multi-layered understanding of short-term financing behaviour among European firms. The results highlight the importance of firm size, industry affiliation and national context in shaping the use and interaction of trade credit and bank loans. By identifying both structural patterns and contextual variability, the study contributes to the broader literature on corporate finance and offers a robust analytical basis for future research and policy development in the field of corporate short-term financial strategies.

In light of the institutional diversity and regulatory heterogeneity across Europe, this study highlights the need for appropriate policy responses that reflect national differences while promoting greater harmonisation in credit markets. Future policy frameworks at the EU level should aim to enhance financial inclusion, particularly for SMEs, by reducing information asymmetries, strengthening creditor protection and improving access to cross-border financing instruments. Moreover, firms operating in different national contexts would benefit from clearer guidance on addressing institutional variability, enabling them to optimise their short-term financing strategies in line with both local market conditions and EU-wide standards. These insights suggest that EU policymakers should prioritise reducing disparities in credit access conditions and promote frameworks that enable firms of different sizes and sectors to adopt financing strategies appropriate to their operational realities and institutional environments.

Index

Note: Page numbers in **bold** and *italics*, refer to tables and figures, respectively.

Abdulla, Y. 45
Adebayo, O. 49
advance payments 76
Afrifa, G. A. **31**
Agostino, M. 15, **28**
Aguiar-Díaz, I. 41
Akashi, K. **30**
Al-Abri, A. 46
Alarcón, L. S. **27**
Al-Hadi, A. 46
Andrieu, G. **27–28**, **73**
Arellano robustness test 84
artificial intelligence 15
asset-backed lending 37
asset-liability adjustments 48
asset structures 37
asymmetric information 31
autocorrelation 85

BACH (Bank for the Accounts of Companies Harmonised) database 66–67; categories 67; data selection 69; dependent variables **70**, 71; variables 70
bank–firm relationships 16
bank loans 2, **6**, **30**, 39
bankruptcy laws 40
Bărbuţă-Mişu, N. **70**
bargaining power 2, 29, 36
Basel Committee 44
Basel III reforms 44
Beck, T. 26, **27**, 28
Biais, B. 7, 23
Białek-Jaworska, A. **30**, **72**
blockchain 15
Bougheas, S. **30**, 36
Breusch, T.S. 83
bridge loans 22
Burkart, M. 7

Cai, G. **30**
Canto-Cuevas, F. J. **26**, **30**, 36, 71
capital-intensive industries 37–39, 46
Carletti, E. 48
Carvalho, C.J. de **27**
cash at hand **72**
cash flow 12
central bank monetary policies 21
Chen, X. **30**
Chodorow-Reich, G, 36
Chou, J. H. **30**, **70**, **72**
Cole, R. A. **27**
collateral 4, **72**
commercial bank loans 2
commercial paper 2–3, **6**
complementarity hypothesis **27–28**
contract enforcement 40
corporate financial management 47
corporate short-term financing 29, 43, 81; decisions 111; *see also* short-term financing
corporate short-term financing Europe: across countries 113–117;

across industries 117–121; across size groups of firms 108–113; complementary *vs.* substitution effect between trade credit and bank loan 99–108; statistics of 89–99
Corporate Sustainability Reporting Directive 50
Costa, T. 47
costs of goods **72**
country effect 40
country effect in trade credit strategies **42**
country-related factors 119
country-specific financial environment 28
COVID-19 pandemic 15, 43–44, 47, 49
credit agreements 104
credit allocation within industries 39
credit infrastructure 41
credit insurance practices 76
credit line functions 22
credit market 39
creditor protection 40
credit policy approach **42**
credit rationing theory 31
credit tightening 37
creditworthiness 10, 13, 19, 29, 77
cross-border challenges **42**
cross-country similarity index **116**
cultural adaptation **42**
Cuñat, V. **27**
Cunningham, R. M. **30**
customers' creditworthiness 7

Dang, V. A. 45
da Silva, **72**
data and credit assessment **42**
debt instrument 2
debtor–creditor relationships 104
debt ratios **72**, 89
debt-to-equity ratios 19
decision-making structure **42**
Deloof, M. **27**
Demirgüç-Kunt, A. 26, **27**, 28, 45
Dewally, M. 46
digital lending platforms 48
digital trade finance solutions 11
Ding, F. 47
Di-Pietro, F. **26**, **30**, 36, 71
Duchin, R. 47
Duliniec, A. **26**
dummy variables **73**

economic crises 15
economic stability 21
Eleftheriou, K. **27**
Ellingsen, T. 7
Environmental, Social, and Governance (ESG) orientation 46
equity financing 78
European Committee of Central Balance Sheet Data Offices (ECCBSOs) 66

factoring 3, **6**, 22
Ferris, J. S. 7
financial capacity 113
financial crises, 2008 5, 15, 37, 43
financial distress 12, 14
financial flexibility 23–24
financial stability 106; of firms 77
financial transparency 31
financing advantage 7
financing preferences 31
firm–bank relationships 21
firm size 31
firm-specific determinants of trade credit **32–35**; cash holdings **33**; collateral **32**; cost of goods sold **33–34**; inventory **32–33**; leverage **34**; operational efficiency **35**; profitability **34–35**
firm-specific financial ratios **72**
Fisman, R. **27**
fixed effects (FE) model 81
formal bank credit availability 8
formal financing 14
Frank, M. Z **27**, **30**
Fukuda, S.I. **30**

geopolitical tensions 49
Ghulam, Y. 36
global financial crisis (GFC) 4
globalisation 79
Gollier, C. 7, 23

Hakro, A. N. 36
Hausman, J. A. 84
Hausman test 99
heteroscedasticity 85
Hogan, T. **70**, **72**
Howorth, C. 36
Hundal, S. 45
Huyghebaert, N. 14

Illueca, M. **30–31**
industrialisation 11
industry-related cash flow volatility 38
industry-specific characteristics 37
industry-specific financing practices 105
industry-specific payment guarantees 76
industry-specific risks 115
inflation rates 21
informal credit assessment 13
informal lending 4–5, **6**
instalment-based credit terms 76
institutional credit 35
institutional risk management **42**
inventory **72**
invoice discounting 22
Ivashina, V. 43–44

Kasuya, M. **30**
Khurshed, A. 45

Lagrange Multiplier test 83
La Rocca, M. **27**
Lavín Fernández, A. 46
Lawrenz, J. **26**, **72**
legal system efficiency 36
Lehman Brothers, collapse of 43
Levine, R. **26**
Lin, C. **26**
Lin, T. T. **30**, **70**, **72**
lines of credit 2
liquidity 5, 16, 23; risks 3
liquidity coverage ratio (LCR) 44
liquidity management 12; strategies 24, 29; tool 18
Liu, G.Q. 48
Liu, P. 46
long-term financing 1
long-term funding structures 44
Love, I. **27**

Ma, L. **28**
Ma, S. **28**
Maksimovic, V. 26, **27**, 28, **30**
market competition 113
market integration 79
Marotta, G. **27**, **30**
Martinez Peria, M.S. 45
Mateut, S. **30**, 36
matrix of correlations for total sample **98**
Mazza, C. 46
McGuinness, G. **70**, **72**
McMillan, J. **27**
mean values of trade credit ratios: across countries *92*; across industries *95*; across size classes *91*; across time *97*
mean values of variables: across countries **92**; across industries **94**
medium-sized companies 67, 89
medium-sized firms 106
Meltzer, A. H. 7, 23
Mizen, P. **30**, 36
money market funds (MMFs) 3–4, **6**
Mruk, E. 41
multinational corporations (MNCs) 41

NACE (Nomenclature statistique des Activités économiques dans la Communauté Européenne) classification 67; industrial sections **68**
Naumani, O. 36
Nehrebecka, N. **30**, **72**
Net Stable Funding Ratio (NSFR) 44
net trade credit (NTC) **70**, 84, 89, 126
Ng, C.K. 24, 37
Nilsen, J. H. 7
non-recourse factoring 3
Norden, L. **30–31**

Oberndorfer, J. **26**, **72**
Öhman, P. **28**

Ono, M. **27**
ordinary least squares (OLS) 83
overdrafts 2
Ozbas, O. 47

Pagan, A.R. 83
Palacín-Sánchez, M. **26**, **30**, 36, 71
Pandemic Emergency Purchase Programme (PEPP) 47
panel regression 99
panel regression models for total sample **100–101**
Panetsidou, S. 47
Pattnaik, D. 43
pecking order theory 31, 36
Peel, M. J. 36
Petersen, M. 7, 24
Pinto, A.P.S. **26**, 71, **72**
Pinto, J. 47
Powell, R. **70**, **72**
price discrimination theories 7
private credit 4, **6**
profitability metrics 19
Psillaki, M. **27**

Rajan, R. 7, 24
Ramdhan, N. 48
random effects (REs) model 82
Raturi, M. **27**
recourse factoring 3
regulatory and tax frameworks 40–41
return on assets **72**
revenue stability 37
reverse factoring 18
risk assessments from suppliers 113
risk- based pricing models 36
risk perception 31
risk profiles 37
Ruiz-Mallorquí, M.V. 41

Sandstrom, A. 45
Santos, J. **27**
Scharfstein, D. 43–44
Schiozer, R. **27**
Sensoy, B.A. 47
service-based firms 21
Shao, Y. 46
short-term bank financing 36, 71
short-term bank loans (BKL) *8–9*, 18, 71, **72**, 73–74, 99, 102, 107; availability of 19; factors affecting availability **20**
short-term financing 123; determinants of 29–41; financial liquidity management 41–50; options **6**; overview 1; short-term bank loans 18–29; sources 1–7; trade credit in 7–18, 23–29
short-termism 50
short-term liquidity 38, 74
short-term liquidity forecasting 16
Silva, A. **27**
size classes, mean values of variables across **90**
size groups of firms **72**
small and medium- sized enterprises (SMEs) 2, 17, 36
small companies 67
Smith, J.K. 24, 37
Smith, R.L. 24, 37
Staglianò, R. **27–28**, **73**
strategic liquidity management 31
structural imbalance 50
substitution hypothesis 24, **25–26**, 35
supplier–buyer relationships 17, 112
supply chain dependencies 21
supply chain dynamics 37
supply chain financing 14, 18
supranational policies 41
Świda, N. **26**
Synapis, A. 47

Taketa, K. **27**
Targeted longer-term refinancing operations (TLTROIII) 48
temporary suspension of debt repayments 47
term loans 2
total asset turnover **72**
trade credit 1–2, **6**, 7–18, *8–9*, 13, 23–29, **30**, 35, 39, 71, 73–74, 84, **103**, 112; bank loan **27–28**; countries **103**; decisions 75; dual role in corporate finance **11**; geographically 17; industries **103**;

liquidity and signalling roles 16; measures 79, **108**; monitoring mechanism 14; patterns 93–94; ratio 10; size *versus* country effect in **118**
trade credit granted (REC) 126
Trade credit obtained (PAY) **70**, 126
Trade credit provided (REC) **70**
trade credit *vs.* short-term bank loan: data characteristics 66–69; definition of variables 69–71; hypotheses' development 71–81; research methods 81–87
trade finance tools used **42**
trade credit received 84
transaction cost 7
Tressel, T. 45
Trivieri, F. 15, **28**

Udell, G.F. **27**
Uesugi, I. **27**
Uskumbayeva, A. 45

Vaidya, R. **27**
van der Zwan, P. **27–28**
Van Kampen, S. **30–31**
variance inflation factor (VIF) 97
for total sample **99**
vriable inclusion in models estimated for various object groups **86**

Wang, S.H. 48
Wang, X. **26**
Wilson, N. 36
Woodruff, C. **27**

Xiao, Z. **30**
Xie, W. **26**

Yamashiro, G. **27**
Yang, X. **30**
Yazdanfar, D. **28**

Zaidi, R. **27**
Zhang, Y. 46
Zwan, P. van der **73**

For Product Safety Concerns and Information please contact our EU representative GPSR@taylorandfrancis.com Taylor & Francis Verlag GmbH, Kaufingerstraße 24, 80331 München, Germany

Printed and bound by CPI Group (UK) Ltd, Croydon, CR0 4YY

14/09/2026

02216243-0015